Bellingham British Columbia Railroad

Builder of Whatcom County

Michael G. Impero

This book is dedicated to:

SUSIE IMPERO: My Wife and Partner in Everything

To all of those who helped in creating *Bellingham Bay and British Columbia Railroad - Builder of Whatcom County*

Special Thanks

PETER RASMUSSEN spent an unbelievable amount of time proof-reading this book. I should have had him as my fourth and fifth grade teacher.

DALE JONES opened his knowledge and picture collection which were enormous help in creating this book. To the best of my knowledge, he is the regional early railroad history expert of Whatcom County.

Thanks

Rose Nerad
Eric Erickson
Wes Gannaway
Dave Robson
Ted Schnepf
Jerry Tegarden
Whatcom Museum - Jeff Jewel
Washington State Archives - Regional Branch - Allison Costanza
Western Washington University CPNWS - Ruth Steele
Whatcom County Assessor - Scott Sandel

Table of Contents

Table of Contents

continued

Chapter 1

Birth of Bellingham Bay and British Columbia Railroad

Industry in Whatcom County was launched with the story of Henry Roeder and Russell Peabody on December 15, 1852, landing at the foot of the waterfront at the future site of Sehome, Washington. At that time, the whole area bordering Puget Sound had the appearance of a continuous forest reaching as far as the eye could see. The coastal plains and the foothills of the Cascade Mountains were covered with virgin timber: Douglas fir, western red cedar, and spruce all in enormous size. The California gold rush had stimulated the Northwest lumber production. Roeder's Whatcom Falls provided the power for a mill, nature provided raw materials, and Bellingham Bay provided the necessary transportation facilities to the California market.

Future industrial development began in 1853 with the discovery of coal in the root hole of a large blown down cedar tree. It was found on Henry Roeder's Donation Land Claim right on the bluff over the beach just west of Elk Street [State Street] and a bit south of what is now Laurel Street. The vein proved to be 17 feet thick lying at a sharp angle to the west under the waters of Bellingham Bay.

Roeder promptly mined 60 tons and shipped it off to a coal hungry San Francisco. With power of attorney to sell the mine and the coal at a value of $18.00 per ton, the mine with the land claim was sold to Fauntleroy, Calhoun, and Benham who organized the Bellingham Bay Coal Mine.

With the uncovering of this coal on the shores of Bellingham Bay, the small struggling towns identified as Sehome and Whatcom were given a tremendous economic boost.

Following the discovery, a California syndicate was formed in San Francisco that procured a vast amount of the land around the coal site. Multiple problems of gas, flooding, a serious fire in 1867, and then a second in 1868, caused tremendous damage to the operation. The economy of the bay collapsed and only five families remained in Sehome. The owners quickly restored the operation and in a short period of time were producing 1400 tons of coal per month. In 1872 a horse-drawn tramway was constructed from the bunkers to the future site of the Bellingham Bay and British Columbia Railroad (B. B. & B. C.) roundhouse on the cliffs of Sehome Mountain.

Operations continued until 1878 when it was decided to abandon the old Sehome Mine. Since Bellingham Bay was directly above it, the mine was having tremendous difficulties with water. With this closure the area dropped into one of many depressions.

The next big announcement was made in all the local newspapers in 1883. The Canadian Pacific Railroad (C. P. R.) had selected the Fraser River Valley as the last leg of their transcontinental route across Canada. To the people of the Bellingham Bay area this meant a transcontinental connection at last.

Pierre Cornwall and the San Francisco owners of the Sehome Mine saw new hope for their investment on the shores of Bellingham Bay. They decided to build a railroad from Sehome to the C. P. R. tracks at the border, thus making their deep-water wharf and 3700 acres of land a link between the East Coast and Asia.

Pierre Cornwall was born on November 23, 1821, in Delaware County, New York. Upon receiving his education in 1848, he headed toward the Northwest. Word of the California gold discovery, which he received in route, caused him to turn south. After a brief mining experience, he established himself in the trading and estate business at Sutter's Fort, Sacramento.

Moving to San Francisco he became widely identified with shipping, merchandising, real estate, and manufacturing interests. He became manager and president of the Black Diamond Coal Company, successfully mining coal deposits at Mt. Diablo near San Francisco. Next came a very profitable Black Diamond Coal Mine southeast of Seattle.

On June 21, 1883, the Bellingham Bay and British Columbia Railroad (B. B. & B. C.) was incorporated in California with authorized capital stock of $1,000,000. Ownership was closely held; and as late as 1906 there were only 16 stockholders.

Stated purposes of the new corporation were to:

Acquire by purchase all property of the Bellingham Bay Coal Company. The said property is situated on Bellingham Bay, Whatcom County, Washington Territory. This corporation is to construct, equip, and maintain a railroad to be operated by steam power from a point on Bellingham Bay, hence in a northeasterly direction about 34 miles to a point intersecting the line of the Canadian Pacific Railroad in British Columbia; this point being approximately 36 miles easterly from the terminus of said Canadian Railroad on Burrard Inlet.

The seven member Board of Trustees were identified as D. O. Mills, New York; Thos. Bell, San Francisco; J. B. Higgin, San Francisco; A. Hayward, Sam Mateo; Louis McLane, Baltimore; P. B. Cornwall, San Francisco; and S. D. Smith, San Francisco. The original stockholders who purchased stock at $100 per share were D. O. Mills-90 shares-$9000; J. B. Haggin-22 shares-$2200; Thomas Bell-24 shares-$2400; A. Hayward-116 shares-$11,600; Louis MaLane-44 shares-$4400; Robert McLane-15 shares-$1500; P. B. Cornwall-38 shares-$3800; L. P. Smith-1 share-$100.

The address of the B. B. & B. C. was 832 Octavia Street, San Francisco, California.

This group of businessmen from throughout the United States included some of the country's wealthiest.

P. B. Cornwall had been a prominent

Californian since 1849, and had amassed a fortune in coal, shipping, and real estate. His wealth, as rated by those who should know, was perhaps $5 million. He mined the first coal on the Pacific Coast – the Mount Diablo Mine.

Alvinza Hayward was another old-time Californian and best-known as the most extensive mine owner on the coast. He opened one which enjoyed a reputation equal to that of any of the Comstock operations. Hayward and his partner were operating a dozen great gold and silver mines in the Golden State and was worth about $30 million.

H. J. Haggin had amassed a fortune in mining equal to that of Mr. Hayward. He later sold the Anaconda Copper mine for $25 million.

Thomas Bell virtually controlled the Quicksilver market, and in mining and commercial ventures had accumulated a fortune estimated at $5 million.

Lloyd Tevis had made his money in banking and was worth $20 million.

A large corps of surveyors started laying out the Bellingham Bay Coal Company's land at Sehome preparing for future businesses. Another corps of engineers made preliminary studies for the new Bellingham Bay and British Columbia Railroad. One intention of the Bellingham Bay Coal Company was to open their extensive coal lands here and ship the valuable resource by rail and water. The excellent shipping facilities, with a fine harbor and a deep channel to the sea, gave routes that offered transportation to any other point on Puget Sound.

Pierre Cornwall arrived July 18, 1883, for the first time for a preliminary inspection of the area. The initial route north to Sumas was to follow the original old Telegraph Road of 1859. One of the main subjects was selecting a point for the railroad to cross the Nooksack River. Cornwall returned to San Francisco on August 27 and came back north again later that year.

Although he had been at the site for only three weeks, construction was underway prior to his returning to California. Grading had begun at the initial point in Sehome-New Whatcom, and work was to be accelerated when more laborers were obtained. Also, before Cornwall returned to California, he had engaged E. C. Plates to survey the town of New Whatcom. That survey was filed on August 31, 1883, to replace the original 1858 plat of Sehome. The initial point of the new plat began at a boulder with a bolt at the shoreline near the current corner of Bay and Holly Streets. This bolt served as a marker to delineate the boundary between Whatcom and New Whatcom.

The company announced that one of the longest ships afloat was about to sail from Philadelphia on November 10 laden with steel rails to be delivered to Sehome. This voyage was expected to take 20 days for passage, with additional railroad materials following soon thereafter.

Also, a very well-known and prominent businessman of the future was to settle in Sehome. Robert Morse arrived in March 1884. He had met Cornwall on the dock in San Francisco in 1883, and they enjoyed talking about the booming West. Mr. Morse was invited by Cornwall to accompany him on one of his trips to Bellingham Bay. It was highly likely that on this special steamer trip in October 1883, Mr. Cornwall offered Morse the position of manager of their interests there. However, Morse opted for starting a general private hardware business. In five months, he landed in New Whatcom with his family and the basic provisions for stocking a warehouse store. Morse lived from 1858 to 1920.

As of September 28, 1883, it was reported that a labor force of 107 men was working on various B. B. & B. C. projects.

At a future time the board members would elect to create a new organization identified as the Bellingham Bay Improvement Company (B. B. I. C.). Many of the assets of the B. B. & B. C. were transferred into this company, including landholdings, mineral rights, timberlands, and sawmills.

Chapter 2
Sehome Wharf and Freight Depot

The grade at sea level began at the Sehome Wharf, extended up a heavy slope along the bluff over the abandoned Sehome Mine, and finally rose to the present corner of Railroad Avenue and Maple Street. At this point the grade flattened and headed north to Whatcom Creek, creating what is today's Railroad Avenue. Sehome's principle roadway was Elk Street [State Street], and the broad Railroad Avenue right of way created a new one to the west.

A local workforce of approximately 40 to 50 men immediately went to work on the waterfront of Bellingham Bay.

BELLINGHAM BAY AND BRITISH COLUMBIA PILEDRIVER
The company would have had several piledrivers depending upon the number of structures that were to be supported by piling. They were normally mounted to a wood sled structure which could have been dragged from one location to the next or mounted on a flat railroad car as a fixed unit. (E. Erickson)

The first item was to construct a scow on which a piledriver could be mounted. Upon the completion of the piledriving, they set to work constructing a wharf extending into deep water with a 200-foot frontage. As soon as the initial work was completed, a schooner by the name of Granger delivered 100,000 board feet of lumber to be used in completing its construction.

In the summer of 1883, there was tremendous railroad activity in Sehome. Surveyors were busy laying out the line and graders worked clearing the new township of Sehome. The new wharf was progressing rapidly.

By the winter of 1883 almost all the construction on the railroad project had stopped. In April 1884 the building of the little road would continue.

SEHOME WATERFRONT, 1919
This cluster of structures illustrates the activity on the Sehome waterfront. In the photo one can see railroad structures, dock, and buildings. (T. Schnepf)

WATERFRONT WAREHOUSE AT END OF SEHOME DOCK
This 1919 waterfront warehouse provided ship access and loading on the right and train access with loading on the left. (T. Schnepf)

SEHOME DOCK
While at the same location, the previous picture was taken in 1919, and this one is obviously much later. The trolley has two coaches delivering people to the dock, the railroad has railroad cars ready to be loaded onto a barge for water shipment south, and at least two or three vessels are tied up at the dock. (W. Gannaway)

MOTOR CAR REPAIR SHOP
This picture again was taken in 1919, and the structure appears to be on solid ground. (T. Schnepf)

MORSE HARDWARE COMPANY
To the right of Morse Hardware was the B. B. & B. C. pattern shop. The Morse Building was the first big complex at the end of State Street and provided hardware goods to the county for over 100 years. (T. Schnepf)

MORSE HARDWARE'S EARLY DELIVERY SERVICE
Morse Hardware and Bellingham Hardware were two of the leading hardware stores in early Bellingham. (Galen Biery Collection - Laura Jacoby)

Chapter 3
Mainline and Branch Line Construction

Mrs. H. Hofercamp, wife of Sehome Postmaster Herman Hofercamp, turned the first sod on the first grade for the Bellingham Bay and British Columbia Railroad on April 7, 1884. The grade began at the newly constructed Sehome Wharf and extended up a heavy slope along the cliff over the abandoned

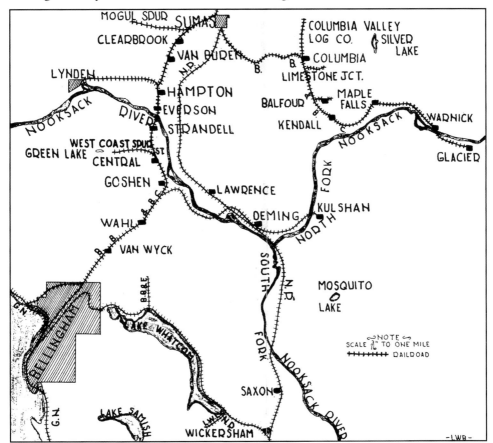

COMPLETE MAP OF THE BELLINGHAM BAY AND BRITISH COLUMBIA RAILROAD

This map illustrates the complete layout of the railroad lines. It shows the mainline from Bellingham to Sumas and Sumas to Glacier, as well as the two branch lines of Hampton to Lynden and Goshen to Kulshan. A few of the spur lines are illustrated; however, the bulk of them are not. (*The Railroad and Locomotive Historical Society, Bulletin No. 84*)

Sehome Mine. It can still be seen paralleling the Parks and Recreation Department's walking trail, passing just west of the Housing Authority building where the railroad roundhouse used to be located. The grade continued its path north to become part of today's Railroad Avenue.

Two miles of track were laid to Whatcom Creek that first year, but work stopped because of a national depression and a slowdown in the Canadian Pacific's westward progress. For the next few years, the construction and organization of the new Bellingham railroad appeared to be in utter chaos most of the time.

In the area of the old Morse Hardware facility, the construction of the shop, roundhouse, and storage buildings was finally taking place. Again, the progress was slow and limited mainly by the total lack of adequate equipment and skilled labor.

In 1888 the Canadian Pacific Railroad (C. P. R.) announced that they would be at the border soon and agreed to connect at Sumas. Cornwall wasted no time.

He had appointed the Reverend I. M. Kalloch, previously mayor of San Francisco, superintendent in 1885. Kalloch retained this post until 1887 when, due to ill health, Alex Van Wyck took it over. Marc L. Strangroom, a prominent California engineer, was then appointed as superintendent and manager, moving to Sehome on May 27, 1888.

Immediately upon his arrival, Strangroom set to the task of determining the lay of the land and the assets of the company. He determined that it owned approximately 3700 acres

in and around Sehome, a small wharf built in 1883, and a railroad that had been graded for three miles with track laid for 1¹/₃ miles to Whatcom Creek.

Two company dwellings were found, an old store, a blacksmith shop, and a few old tools and horses. All had been turned over to Mr. Strangroom by past agent Mr. Van Wyck.

At this time the settlement of Sehome contained not over 50 people; and Whatcom, separated from it by Whatcom Creek and by a half mile of forest, had not more than 300 to 400. Bellingham and Fairhaven, lying on the bay and about two miles south of Sehome, contained perhaps 50 more.

After spending a day studying the situation and making examinations of the country, Strangroom retained a couple of assistant engineers from Seattle, organized an engineer corps, and commenced the survey for a railroad to connect Bellingham Bay with the Canadian Pacific Railway.

A thorough investigation convinced him that the original line planned in 1884 as far as the Nooksack River could be much improved. He abandoned the two miles of grading done north of Whatcom Creek. After much slow, tedious work and running many lines through almost impermeable forest jungle, he developed a line 4000 feet shorter, with better grade and alignment, and costing less than the original estimates for construction. He felt satisfied to have obtained a "first road" at a very moderate cost, considering the country through which it ran.

The engineers and chief officials of the C. P. R. repeatedly told Strangroom that it was equal to or superior to much of their line in every respect; except in the lightness of the rails, planned for 50 lbs. per yard.

By the summer of 1888, Strangroom's crews had strengthened and repaired the old wharf and trestle, and put the roadbed and track through town in good condition. They then commenced clearing and construction beyond Whatcom Creek.

Early winter rains and the short

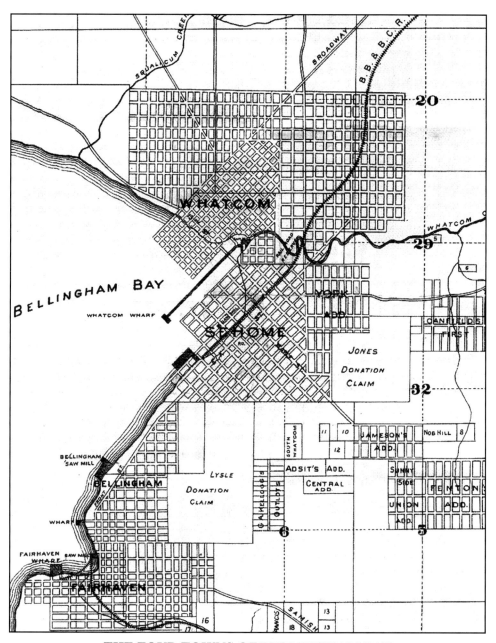

THE FOUR TOWNS OF BELLINGHAM BAY
Whatcom, Sehome, Bellingham, and Fairhaven combined later to become Bellingham. (City of Bellingham)

winter days made it impossible to do more work than immediately necessary. A stop for the winter was made after clearing and grubbing roads and doing other work incidental to the construction. In 1889 work resumed and proceeded with location and construction as fast as circumstances and funds appeared to warrant.

A four-stall roundhouse and turntable and 1³/₄ miles of spur or siding were constructed at New Whatcom. Also, built and operating in conjunction with a phone company, a telephone line ran the whole length of the new road.

Another item viewed upon his arrival was the need of accommodations for new workers as they could not have been able to provide for themselves. To that end the company built 27 plain, but neat and comfortable, cottages containing four or five rooms and costing from $350 to $550 each. They were rented continuously for $8, $10, and $12 per month.

Strangroom, as B. B. & B. C. Superintendent, built the first water system for what was called New Whatcom. In addition, the first electric company and the Bellingham Bay Improvement Company Lumber Mill were constructed at the foot of Cornwall

EARLY SEHOME
The Bellingham Bay and British Columbia Railroad would run toward Whatcom Creek. The identity of the roadway to the right was Elk Street [State Street]. (Exact year of the photo is in question.) (W. Gannaway)

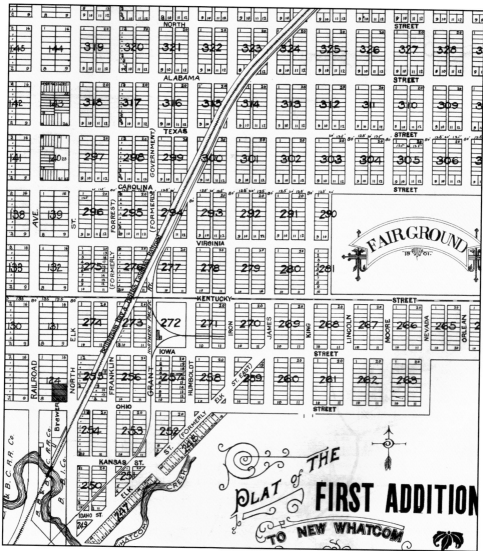

EARLY MAP OF B. B. & B. C. CROSSING NEW WHATCOM
Reviewing this map, one can see the changes to Bellingham. (City of Bellingham)

Avenue. He also supervised real estate operations, mapping, building planked streets and sidewalks in the growing town, and commenced to sell the company's 3700 acres.

Within a few months, the freighter "Germania" arrived in Sehome with 250 tons of rails. By the end of the summer the bridge over Whatcom Creek was nearly complete. However, after the first two miles of track had been laid,

construction lagged once again.

The fall of 1888 marked a turning point for the struggling B. B. & B. C. The old "Germania" again arrived at the dock with two engines, 30 flat cars, and 400 tons of rail. This rolling stock and machinery was formerly the property of the Black Diamond Railroad of California. The engines weighed 36 tons each and had been serviced and overhauled in San Francisco. One engine was named after the patron saint of the company, D. O. Mills, and the other one was called Black Diamond. After one or two weeks of reassembling the machines, the "D. O. Mills," #1, of the B. B. & B. C., became the first locomotive to operate in the Bellingham Bay country on October 11. Shortly thereafter, #2, the "Black Diamond," was placed in operation.

However, both machines' area of operation was very restricted. A favorite story of the old timers was that whenever a boat arrived, the engine's chief use was to run up and down two to three miles of track with much whistling and blowing off steam. This was done in order to impress the visitors with the fact that Bellingham Bay had its own railroad in running condition.

The construction of the railroad continued, and by April 1889 the rail proudly claimed 3¹/₂ miles of track, 4 miles of grading, and 5¹/₂ miles of slashing. The slashing involved the cutting and removal of virgin timber and stumps which ranged up to ten feet in diameter, so one could easily recognize the difficulty. Also, 3 miles of rail was on the grade and 12 miles of rail were in route.

The track reached the Nooksack River in September 1890 and the British Columbia Boundary in March 1891. No gravel or other materials suitable for ballast, except a small quantity of coal cinders from the mine in Whatcom, were found on the grade until reaching the river. The river gravel became the main source from there to the international boundary. By redoing the ballast work back to the south, the entire

"D. O. MILLS" ENGINE
The first engine (Engine #1) arrived in Sehome to be used on the new B. B. & B. C. Railroad. Photo was taken by Fred Jukes in 1902. (D. Hamilton)

line was put in first class condition.

The first thing the B. B. & B. C. Railroad had required was finding the route. Then they prepared the right of way either by direct purchase or leasing. The point of crossing the Nooksack was also of major importance. Once that was selected, primary surveys had to determine design criteria for the route. The grade could not exceed a certain incline of approximately 2.2% and the curves of the bed had to be made to a radius required by engineering standards. Also, the characteristics of the terrain, such as wet swampy land or solid rock hillsides, had to be measured. In the early days of railroad construction, there were few machines that could move earth from one location to another. So, many times, instead of trying to put fill in a low area, they would simply build a wood trestle. Trestles were expensive to build, and they often rerouted the road to avoid the need.

After the preliminary plan was created, the next major function was to determine the ownership of each piece of land and proceed with creating a document that would allow the railroad to cross their land. In the whole length of the mainline from Bellingham to Glacier, one can only make a guesstimate of the number of parcels of land that had to be crossed. In some of these cases, the owner was very openly eager to have the railroad come through his area to provide access, requiring only a $1 lease from the railroad. However, we must realize that in some cases the owners of the land absolutely did not want a railroad to cross it, no matter what the revenue could have been. So again, the railroad had to be rerouted to a different location to bypass those parcels of land.

The number of men involved in searching out ownership and then locating the actual owners would have been exceptionally large. And because the railroad was eager to connect to the British Columbia railroads, it would have been a monumental task. A large amount of letter writing and telegraph messages were needed.

Following are two examples of documents that were created to allow the railroad to proceed. Some of the documents would have been truly short, possibly one paragraph; however, some documents were many pages long.

The B. B. & B. C. main section reached its North Terminus at Sumas on March 6, 1891. In the original plan there were to be no spur tracks laid off this main route. This concept assumed through traffic would be the main purpose of the new railroad tying Bellingham to Sumas and Canada.

On September 18, 1897, the B. B. & B. C. announced the planned branch line from Clearbrook to Lynden. It would open the rich farmland in that area and provide transportation for its products.

Also, the Mt. Baker Mining District had great potential that was being recognized at this time. As an example, the railroad saw a tremendous future in coal development. Up on the mountains above Glacier were large areas of exposed coal.

John Donovan was referred to as JJ Donovan. He was born in Rummey, New Hampshire, on September 8, 1858. His parents, Patrick Donovan and Julia O' Sullivan, were immigrants from Ireland. Patrick and Julia became

GUS BELLMAN & EMMA BELLMAN B.B.B.C. RR CO. RIGHT OF WAY DEED.

   This indenture made this 22nd day of July 1889. Between Gus
Bellman and Emma Bellman his wife of the County of Whatcom in
the Territory of Washington of the first part and the Bellingham
Bay British Columbia Railroad Company a corporation, the party of
the second part Witnesseth, that the said party of the first part
for the purpose of promoting the construction of a railroad in
Whatcom County in said Territory and the sum of one dollar---
in hand paid the receipt whereof is hereby acknowledged, do
hereby grant, bargain, sell and convey to the said party of the
second part, its successors or assigns the right of way for the
construction of said companys railroad, or any part therof, over,
through, under or across, cross lands belonging to said part of
the first part and all rights, title and interess of Whatcom
Nature or kind in and to the same interested in said County
of Whatcom said Territory of Washington to and for the width
of one hundred feet, and for the whole length of the line of
said railroad, through said land or lands, wherever the said
company shall locate or have located the line of said railroad.
Said lands are described as follows, The East half (E) of the
South East Quarter (SE) and the South East Quarter (SE) of the
North East Quarter (NE) of Section three (3) Township Thirty-
eight (38) North Range Three East W.M. (Willamette Merdian).
And the company agrees to make cattleguards wherever a fence
crosses said Railroad either now or here after.

BELLMAN RIGHT OF WAY DEED

Gus Bellman's 160-acre homestead was located about three miles northeast
of the city limits. He had an extensive vegetable farm, orchards, and green-
houses to provide for the needs of the city of Whatcom. It was a complex
farming operation and included the assistance of four of his sons. The
Bellmans were eager to have the railroad travel through their property as
this would provide transportation for their vegetables going into town and
to provide transportation for horse manure for fertilizer coming back out of
town from the Kentucky Street Stables. The railroad gained a 100 foot right of
way through the Bellman property for a total lease amount of $1. (D. Johnson)

13- 398 & 399 (CONT).

This conveyance is absolute and to take effect from and after its execution, but nevertheless in case said company or its successors shall fail to construct its said railroad, and put it into operation upon and over said lands within three years from date, the same shall become null and void. Witness on hands and seals this Twenty-second day of July 1889. Gus Bellman seal, Emma Bellman seal, M.L. Strangroom agt B.B.B.C. RR CO. Signed, sealed and delivered in presence of G.L. Strangroom, Josh S. Walton, Territory of Washington, County of Whatcom is a receipt S. Walton a Notary Public in and for Washington Territory do hereby partake that on this Twenty-seventh day of July A D 1889, personally appeared before me Gus Bellman and Emma Bellman his wife to me known to be the individuals described in and who executed the within instrument and acknowledged that they signed and sealed the same as their free and voluntary act and deed for the uses and purposes therein mentioned, and the said Emma Bellman wife of said Gus Bellman upon an examination by me seperate and apart from her said husband, acknowledged that she there of her own free will and without fear of or concession from her said husband unto the same. Given under my hand and off-

icial seal this Twenty-seventh day of July A D 1889. Josh S. Walton Notary Public in and for Washington Territory. 11:00 A.M. February 6th. 1890.

Hugh Eldridge   B.B.B.C. RR CO.

GUS BELLMAN RIGHT OF WAY DEED PAGE TWO
The document was signed July 27, 1889. Witness Hugh Eldridge signed for
Whatcom County, Washington Territory. (D. Johnson)

ROBERT MCRAE WARRANTY DEED

This McRae Warranty Deed is one of the most abbreviated forms that was found. His land was located at the future town of Kendall, Washington. (CPNWS - Western Washington University)

**ORIGINAL EVERSON BELLINGHAM BAY AND
BRITISH COLUMBIA BRIDGE**

A major winter flood of the Nooksack River destroyed the Everson Bridge in 1900. This pile bent bridge design was not adequate for the rapid floodwaters of the Nooksack. (W. Gannaway)

EVERSON TWO-SPAN BRIDGE
The original bridge was replaced with a modern two-span timber truss bridge. After the bridge was gravely damaged by a fire set by kids, it was destroyed. (Whatcom County Museum)

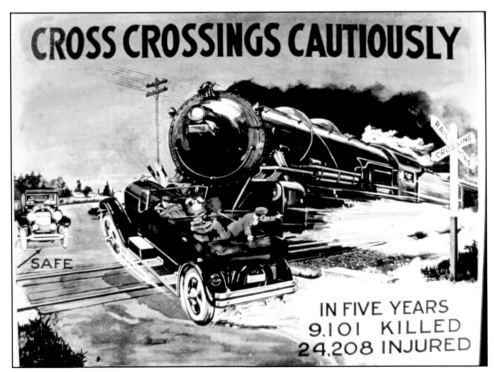

RAILROAD AND HIGHWAY EDUCATION
Since the first "collision" of railroad and highway traffic, railroads have always had the right of way. (Galen Biery Collection - Laura Jacoby)

OBSOLETE RAILROAD CROSSING SIGNAGE
This sign was located on an abandoned track on Cocopah Indian Reservation
land in an Arizona desert. Only with the unbelievable dry weather could this
sign survive the test of time. (S. Dias)

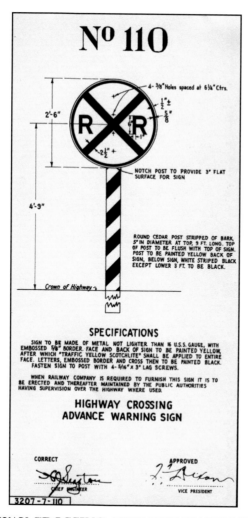

HIGHWAY CROSSING ADVANCE WARNING SIGN

Signage was an important element of railroad construction and in preparing them for operation. Some of the signs were for public safety while many were for the operation of the train. Those illustrated here are not identified for the B. B. & B. C. Railroad as they were signs of the Great Northern. However, all signs on the early railroads would have almost been the same. The installation of railroad signage would have been one of the most important parts of preparing a railroad to operate. (E. Erickson)

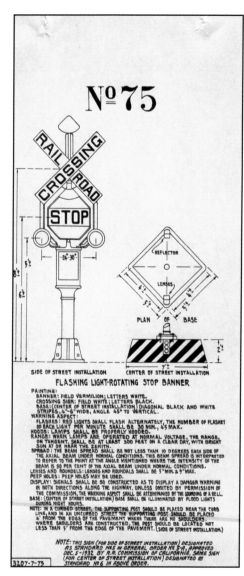

FLASHING LIGHT-ROTATING STOP BANNER

This is a fine example of a street crossing by a railroad. Before the days of electricity it is not known how the lights were illuminated.
(E. Erickson)

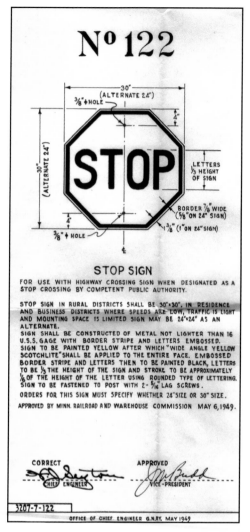

RAILROAD STOP SIGN
Another example of a railroad stop sign at a public road. (E. Erickson)

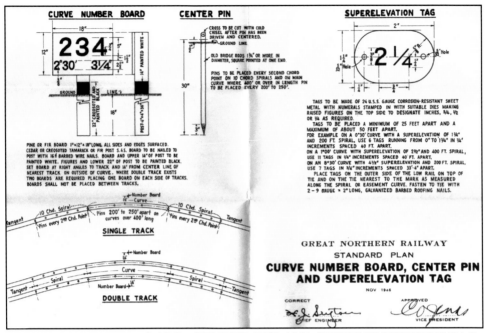

CURVE NUMBER BOARD, CENTER PIN AND SUPERELEVATION TAG

This signage is for the operation of the train and is used by the engineer and other members of the crew. It identifies the curve number, the radius of the turn in degrees, and other valuable information. (E. Erickson)

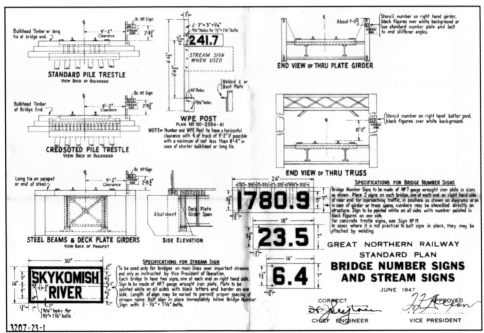

BRIDGE NUMBER SIGNS AND STREAM SIGNS

Another example of a sign that is solely for the use of the engineer and other members of the crew is shown here. (E. Erickson)

SUMAS B. B. & B. C. DEPOT
The depot is situated in the center of the picture directly above the words
"Main Section." To the right of the station is a row of B. B. & B. C. cars.
(D. Jones)

farmers and had seven children with JJ being the oldest.

After the completion of his high school courses, JJ Donovan entered the New Hampshire State Normal School, from which he graduated in 1877. For the following three years he was engaged in civil engineering at the Polytechnic Institute in Worcester, Massachusetts, where he received his B.S. diploma in 1882 with a full degree in civil engineering.

His first job was that of an assistant engineer working for the Northern Pacific Railroad that was about to connect the completed line across the continental United States.

Next, he was transferred to the Cascade Division of the Northern Pacific. His first assignment there was in the area of Prosser, Washington. With completion of that work in 1888, he journeyed back to New England. When he returned to Helena, Montana, in the same year, he was accompanied by his bride, Clara Isabel of Melrose, Massachusetts.

Later in 1888, JJ arrived in the town of Fairhaven which later became a part of Bellingham. His skills were solicited by many companies due to their needs in civil engineering projects in the area. The town consisted of a few dwellings standing in the midst of dense forest and

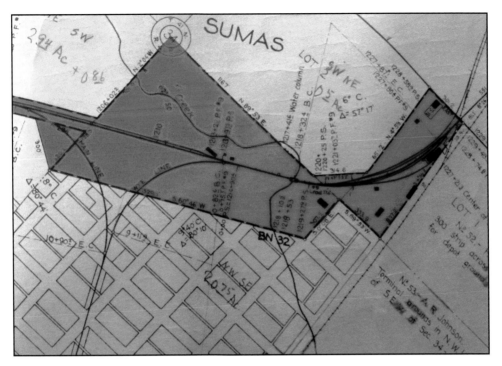

MAP OF B. B. & B. C. RAILROAD IN SUMAS
The mainline from Bellingham enters the map on the upper left area and then makes a sweeping turn to the right at the 'Y' heading for Glacier. The mainline continues in the red area to the Canadian border. Using the previous picture and this picture, one can visualize the border approach. (Whatcom County Assessor)

had a total population on Bellingham Bay of not more than 500. The road between Fairhaven and Whatcom was impassable, and the traffic from one point to the other was mainly by rowboat.

After working for a period of years on various development and railroad construction in the Whatcom County area, he became Chief Engineer of Land Appraisal. Afterwards, he was named Chief Engineer of the Blue Canyon Coal Mining Company and the Bellingham Bay and Eastern Railroad Company, formed by Montana capital in 1891.

In August 1898 Peter Larson, Julius

Bloedel, and JJ Donovan purchased 160 acres of timber on the South Bay and formed the Lake Whatcom Logging Company, each acquiring one third interest in the business. Larson was made president, Donovan became vice president, and Bloedel acted as manager. In 1900 they organized the Larson Lumber Company. In 1901 this group constructed Mill A at Larson (now Bloedel Donovan Park), Mill B in 1907, and later a box factory.

In 1913 the business was reorganized, and the present management style of the Bloedel-Donovan Lumber Company was adopted. Bloedel continued as the president of the corporation and the head of the sales department. He also directed the activities of the mills. For 12 years Donovan filled the office of vice president and oversaw railway operations.

The company acquired a mill and logging plant at Skykomish in 1917, and, in 1920, purchased large logging properties in Clallam County.

Donovan was an influential member of the Catholic Church and reached the Fourth Degree in the Knights of Columbus. He was also highly active in the Republican Party and worked on various occasions as an advisor to the governor. In addition, he was a member of the State Board of Charities and Corrections for some time. For years he served in an advisory capacity to Saint Joseph Hospital in Bellingham and was actively involved with the construction of the new building overlooking Bellingham Bay in 1901.

One of the original eight stockholders, Donovan was involved with the planning, construction, and operation of the original Mount Baker Lodge which opened to the public in 1927. Unfortunately, the beautiful structure burned to the ground in 1931. (See *The Grand Lady of Mount Baker* by Michael G. Impero, 2015)

In 1898 Donovan was made General Superintendent and Chief Engineer of the Bellingham Bay and British Columbia Railroad and the Bellingham Bay Improvement Company, acting in this capacity for eight years. He immediately began survey work to extend the line to Spokane. Also during that period, the corporation and its auxiliaries devoted much time and capital to prospecting for coal

and other minerals, also developing valuable waterpower at Nooksack Falls. Timberlands from Sumas to Glacier provided a great potential market for the railroad with the shipping of raw timber and milled products.

The decision had been reached prior to Donovan being appointed manager that the line would continue from Sumas to Glacier. There were three proposed routes and one of his first responsibilities was reviewing them and giving his recommendations to P. B. Cornwall, President of the Bellingham Bay and British Columbia Railroad in San Francisco.

Route number one via South Pass created some negative calculations. It would require an additional 2.20 miles of construction costing $46,915 more than construction starting at Sumas. Also, it was steep terrain and had 70 feet of added elevation to be gained. With the added elevation gain, it was determined that the tonnage hauled per day would be less on this route.

Donovan's report also identified problems on the Fish (Silver) Lake Route. With a ridge near the shore, the requirement of gaining more elevation to pass around the lake was reviewed. He did not favor the Fish Lake Route.

The third route by way of Columbia Valley became the obvious choice. It was by far the easiest for construction. However, the need for Saar Creek Canyon Bridges posed a problem.

Engineer Estep indicated in a report to Donovan that the cost of the first 15.2 miles would be $162,138. The next 4.9 miles of construction was estimated to cost $54,656, and $5000 would be required for the construction of depots, water tanks, and engine sheds.

JOHN JOSEPH DONOVAN
JJ Donovan, born on September 8,
1858, in New Hampshire, was one
of the most respected businessmen
and citizens in the early history
of Bellingham. He consistently
demonstrated his leadership abilities
with his involvement in many
different business ventures and as
a leader in the community and the
Catholic Church. He died on January
27, 1937, at an age of 78. (*History of*
***Whatcom County, Volume II*)**

In October 1899, the word that all
the people of Columbia Valley, Maple
Falls, and Glacier had been waiting
for was received, the Bellingham Bay
and British Columbia Railroad was
proposing to extend the mainline from
Sumas to Glacier. This branch, possibly
in the future, would also extend easterly
in the direction of Eastern Washington.
Construction of this initial line was
expected to cost about $250,000.

With this announcement there was
great excitement in the area of Keese.
This small pioneer community was the
first settlement up the North Fork on
the Nooksack River and was located
near the mouth of Kendall Creek. In
discussions with planners and surveyors
for the railroad, it became obvious that
the route would not go through this
little community. Many of the local
people had purchased land on what they
felt would be the route. The ones who
picked the future town site of Kendall
made the right choice.

R. S. Lambert, the chairman of the
Sumas committee which was assisting
in securing the right of way through
the town for the new road, reported it
practically almost obtained. There were
only one or two parties with whom the
negotiations were not closed, but he
stated it would be done by the following
Monday. Lambert, an attorney, enjoyed
a large amount of respect in the
community, having served as the mayor
of Sumas, in offices for Whatcom
County Government, and in Olympia as
a state representative.

His biggest claim to fame, however,
was in a totally different field. He, with
Jack Post and Luman Van Valkenburg,
discovered the rich gold mine named
"The Lone Jack." This created the Mount
Baker Gold Rush and the mountain
community of Shuksan. (See *The Lone
Jack* by Michael G. Impero, 2007)

Published in the legal paper of
Whatcom County, *The Blade*, on
November 21, 1899, was the first
bid call requesting proposals for the
construction of this branch.

*Sealed proposals for the clearing,
grubbing, grading and culverts on
ten miles of railroad from Sumas
eastward will be received until noon,*

Tuesday, December 12, 1899, at the office of the B. B. & B. C. Railroad, New Whatcom, Washington. Each bid must be accompanied by a certified check for $500. For further particulars, apply at the office of the company to JJ Donovan, General Superintendent, B. B. & B. C. Railroad, New Whatcom, Washington, November 18, 1899.

Engineer Lyle and his party surveyed from Sumas to Boulder Creek. Its first section was from Sumas to ten miles up the route. They set up camp at the Nicoey Place in Saar Creek Canyon. By February, the surveying crew was planning to have the route laid out to Cornell, later renamed Glacier.,

From Sumas the proposed line climbed to Hilltop Siding, in the vicinity of Columbia, on various grades, with the maximum being 3.19%. The 3.19 grade was extremely steep and if it could be lower, it would be done.

In November, Contractor J. G. Fairfowl, who received the first contract of the railroad construction work, was assuring JJ that he would be finished with more than the first four miles of road by December 17. He employed 64 men and 20 teams of horses. After a little over five weeks' work had been put in on the line, the result was that the entire route, excepting about 1800 feet, had been cleared. Two miles of the road was ready for track, and a half mile more was almost finished. The track layers would be at work within ten days as rails, spikes, and fasteners had already arrived in part. In all, about 1500 rails, each 30 feet long and weighing 1800 pounds, a total of 2,700,000 pounds or 1350 tons, or 17 carloads of about 80 tons each. The number of rails to the mile was 352.

When the Honorable R. S. Lambert, Mayor of Sumas, was in Whatcom he announced that the B. B. & B. C. had just received five carloads of rails for the extension from Sumas. Also, the parties who owned the limestone quarry in the Columbia Valley intended to develop the property and would manufacture both lime and cement.

Superintendent Donovan reported to *The Blade* newspaper that 1900 was a highly successful year for the railroad and gave the following report:

Work on B. B. & B. C. extension from Sumas toward the North Fork was commenced last April on the first contract of ten miles of track, including a 'Y' and track run to the new McNair mill, completing it in May. Contractor J. G. Fairfowl had cleared and graded those first miles. J. A. Moore of the city completed the masonry on the steel bridge across Saar Creek in the canyon.

The material for the new steel bridge is expected about November 23. It is being made in the East by the Pacific Bridge Company of Portland Oregon. It will be unloaded at Sumas and when the track reaches the bridge site, it will be put on cars and taken out. There are five wooden bridges to be built before reaching the steel bridge. These, together with ten other bridges, will be contracted within a few weeks and we expect to build all on the end of the track. The piling has already been delivered for most of the bridges and the lumber will be furnished by the Bellingham Bay Improvement Company (B. B. I. C.). The labor and iron will be furnished by the contractor.

J. G. Fairfowl is now working on the second contract from Kendall Creek to Maple Creek and is expecting that it

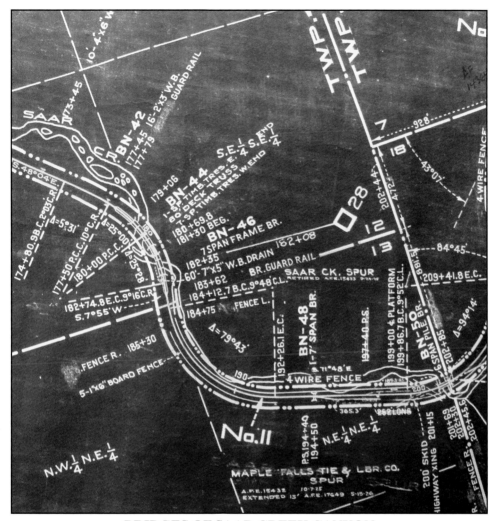

BRIDGES OF SAAR CREEK CANYON
This rail line within Saar Creek Canyon was the most difficult to construct on the Glacier Branch. All the work was performed within the walls of the canyon with four bridges being erected, including the steel bridge BN-44. (Whatcom County Assessor)

LARGEST TIMBER TRESTLE IN SAAR CREEK CANYON
This existing massive wood structure is 70 feet high and 500 feet long. (M. Impero)

ANOTHER VIEW OF THE SAAR CREEK BRIDGE
This three-decker structure required 250,000 board feet of lumber and was estimated to cost $4000. Superintendent Donovan calculated that this bridge could be built in two weeks. (M. Impero)

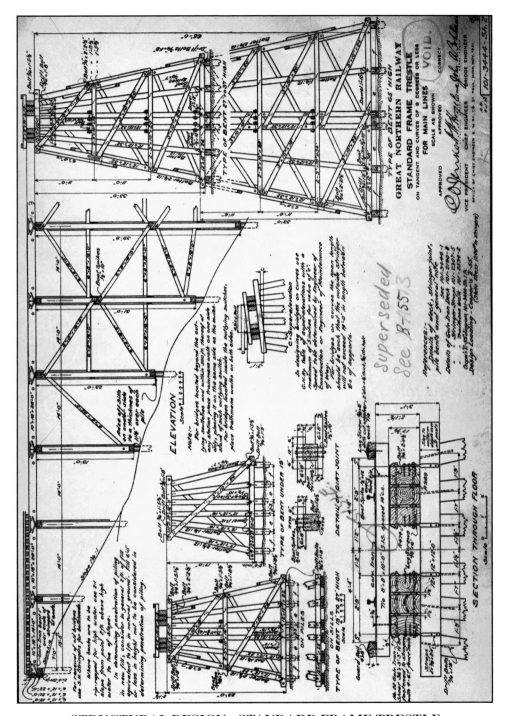

STRUCTURAL DESIGN - STANDARD FRAME TRESTLE
This is not a B. B. & B. C. Railroad design but one from the Great Northern
Railroad. They would have been similar in either case. One cannot
comprehend the amount of weight that was applied with a fully loaded train
on this trestle. (E. Erickson)

STEEL BRIDGE CROSSING SAAR CREEK
This bridge was the only steel one constructed on the Bellingham Bay and British Columbia Railroad. The bridge was ordered from Pacific Bridge Company of Portland, Oregon. (M. Impero)

STEEL BRIDGE CROSSING SAAR CREEK
The above crossing was made using the steel bridge and a timber trestle bridge. Three quarters of the way across the span, the section was straight. The remaining curved section of the bridge was timber trestle. (M. Impero)

MASONRY BRIDGE PIER
This bridge pier and the bridge pier at the Warnick Bridge were both of
masonry construction. These blocks were created from native stone and then
laid up in this manner. Note the remarkable workmanship. (M. Impero)

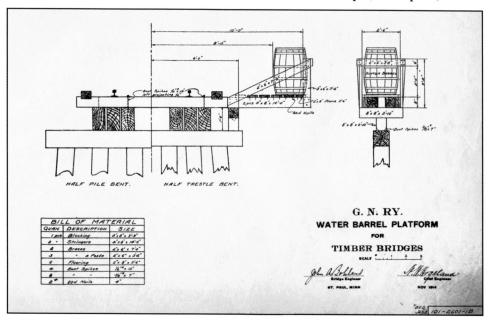

TYPICAL FIRE WATER BARREL PLATFORM
Water barrels with buckets were provided on all bridges and trestles of
a certain length and beyond. The spacing of the water barrels across the
structure varied. (E. Erickson)

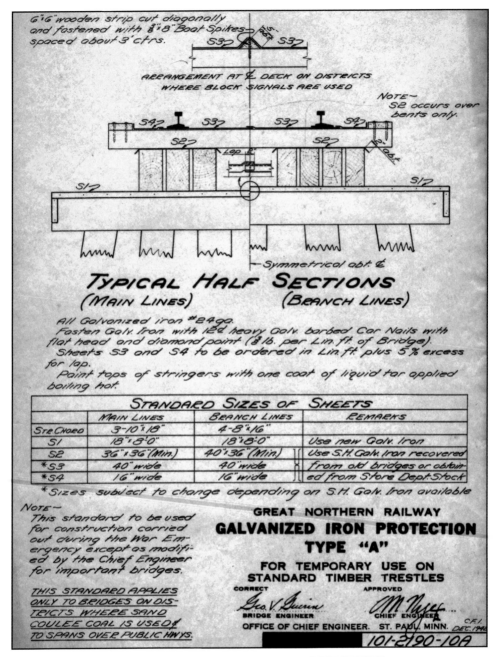

Standard Sizes of Sheets

	Main Lines	Branch Lines	Remarks
Str. Chord	3-10"×18"	4-8"×16"	
S1	18"×8'0"	18"×8'0"	Use new Galv. Iron
S2	36"×36" (Min.)	40"×36" (Min.)	Use S.H. Galv. Iron recovered
*S3	40" wide	40" wide	from old bridges or obtain-
*S4	16" wide	16" wide	ed from Store Dept. Stock

*Sizes subject to change depending on S.H. Galv. Iron available

NOTE~
This standard to be used for construction carried out during the War Emergency except as modified by the Chief Engineer for important bridges.

THIS STANDARD APPLIES ONLY TO BRIDGES ON DISTRICTS WHERE SAND COULEE COAL IS USED & TO SPANS OVER PUBLIC HWYS.

GREAT NORTHERN RAILWAY
GALVANIZED IRON PROTECTION
TYPE "A"

FOR TEMPORARY USE ON
STANDARD TIMBER TRESTLES

CORRECT
Geo. V. Guinn
BRIDGE ENGINEER
OFFICE OF CHIEF ENGINEER.

APPROVED
C. F. I.
CHIEF ENGINEER
ST. PAUL, MINN. DEC. 1943

101-2190-10A

GALVANIZED IRON FIRE PROTECTION
This fire protection was used on timber trestles. Again, this is a Great Northern design and it is not known if B. B. & B. C. used this process. (E. Erickson)

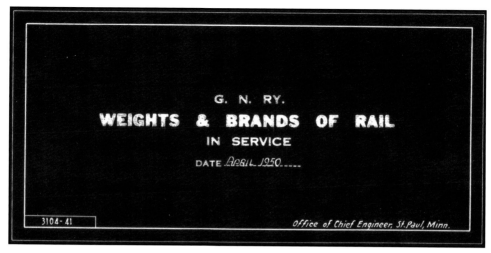

G. N. RY.

WEIGHTS & BRANDS OF RAIL

IN SERVICE

DATE _April 1950_

3104-41

Office of Chief Engineer, St.Paul, Minn.

MANUFACTURER'S RAIL HANDBOOK

The Manufacturer's Rail Handbook listed the manufacturers of railroad rail and gave all the physical dimensions. Different weight rails were used in different locations such as mainline, quality spurs, and logging spurs. All given weights for the rail were the weight per three feet. A 60-pound rail weighed 20 pounds per foot. (E. Erickson)

Weight Per Yard	Section	Brand and Year Rolled		Base	Height	Web	Head
		BESSEMER STEEL					
75#	StPM&M 75#/87	JOLIET STEEL CO. 548	1888	4-1/2"	4-3/4"	1/2"	2-1/2
	"	G.N.LINE 7501 ILLINOIS STEEL CO. UNION	1892				
75#	GN 75/93	G.N.LINE 77501 ILL.STEEL CO. 1898-99 PENN.STEEL, 55 WKS. 1901-02	1893	4-3/4"	5"	9/16"	2-7/1
	"	G.N.LINE 7507 ILLINOIS STEEL CO. SO. WKS.	1893- 4-5				
	GN 75/96	937 LORAIN STEEL CO. LORAIN, O. 1903 G.N.LINE 7509 ILLINOIS STEEL CO. SO. WKS. UNION	1896- 7-8	5"	5"	9/16"	2-19/
	"	THE JOHNSON CO. LORAIN, O. MADE IN U.S.A.	1898				
	"	CARNEGIE, E.T.	1898				

TYPICAL HANDBOOK PAGE

This page shows the weight and physical dimensions of rail. When the railroad boom was crossing the United States, hundreds of rail manufacturers appeared overnight. (E. Erickson)

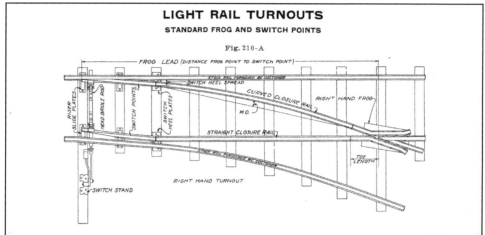

LIGHT RAIL TURNOUTS
STANDARD FROG AND SWITCH POINTS

Fig. 210-A

Cut shows turnout such as is ordinarily used with straight frog and switch points, the curved closure rail being tangent to these parts.

A complete turnout consists of one frog, one split switch, one pair of closure rails drilled and one switch stand.

Closure rails or switch stands can be omitted.

We list below Frogs and Split Switches for these turnouts. Switch Stands listed on page 209.

When ordering or inquiring for prices, specify the weight rail, track gauge and the frog number or frog lead, and specify whether or not closure rails or switch stands are desired. Specify type of stand.

For the smaller frog numbers and narrower track gauges we suggest the use of a curved frog turnout with switch points abutting the frog wing rail.

MECHANISM OF A RAIL SWITCH

A complete turnout consisted of one frog, one split switch, one pair of drilled closure rails, and one switch stand. (E. Erickson-Hendrie & Bolthoff Mfg. & Supply, p. 210)

MECHANISM OF RAIL SWITCH
Moving the lever in the lower part of the picture from left to right changes the direction of the train. (M. Impero)

NORMAL RAILROAD RIGHT OF WAY

The land where the right of way penetrated held a variety of different conditions. In some cases, it was over lakes and streams, marshy land, and as shown in the above picture, through virgin timberland. The right of way was cleared to a width of 80 to 100 feet, with 100 feet being the normal. Who became the owner of the felled and bucked timber? William Warnick took the picture in 1900. (Whatcom County Museum)

RAILROAD CONSTRUCTION TRAIN

The construction train followed as closely as possible behind the completed track. The machine moved forward all the materials as required, as well as the men and the camp. (Whatcom County Museum)

GRADE CHECKER

The grade checker was a particularly important individual in laying out the railroad. It was his job to constantly be checking that the required grade of the railroad was not excessive. If this amount were too much the engine would have difficulties in climbing the grade. Also, if it were too steep, the coming down could create a runaway. The picture was taken in 1900 by William Warnick, construction engineer. (Whatcom County Museum)

RAILROAD CUT THROUGH HILLS

As the picture illustrates, railroad material handling cars were loaded by hand; and then the horses backed up and pulled the cars to an unloading spot. The railroad rails shown here were strictly temporary and would be removed for the final rail. (Whatcom County Museum)

BELLINGHAM BAY AND BRITISH COLUMBIA STEAM SHOVEL

Looking at available records, there appeared to be only one steam shovel in the early stages. This machine was not available in the very beginning, but later played a big part in construction. Notice the two-man operation and no steel cables, only steel chains. Years after the power source was replaced with diesel and gasoline motors they were still referred to as steam shovels. (D. Jones)

LATER VERSION OF A STEAM SHOVEL

This is an independent tracked machine and probably diesel powered. In this photo you can identify steel rods being used to establish grade and width. Also, if you look in the background you can see what appears to be a cookhouse. The man in the doorway with a white apron appears to be the cook. Notice the pots and pans hanging on the wall. (E. Erickson)

will be completed within six weeks. We expect to have trains running over the new road before Christmas. It is not yet definitely determined, but we expect at some time in the future to build the road beyond Maple Creek.

The expenditures of the construction, including steel, from Sumas to Kendall this year amount to $250,000.

JJ Donovan made public the following report:

On the mainline this year we have replaced the bridge at Everson, which was washed away, with a new span and have put protection work around the bridge. We have sent out a piledriver and 130 more piles at the head of Kale's Slough. This additional work will put that in shape for the winter better than ever before. All other bridges on the line have been thoroughly repaired during the past month. We have completed the laying in of ballast which was started last year and now the track is in better shape than it has been for the past five years. Over 12,000 new ties have been put between the city and Sumas. All the depot buildings, except for New Whatcom and Wahl which were repainted just last year, having been repainted and revamped. These include Goshen, Millerton, Everson, and Sumas. The work was done by H. H. Hill of this city.

The work on the Everson bridge was done by Pacific Bridge Company, the repair work by George C. Blakeslee, the track repairing by J. A. Mosby of Sumas in conjunction with the section foremen, Wm. McDonald of Everson, J. Wheeler of Goshen and M. Burns of New Whatcom.

In the city we have overhauled the yard, put in a new switcher, and built a new log dump and a passing track at the mill; so that now the log trains go down with the Engine #1 ahead and also increase the size of the transfer track with the Great Northern at the mill. A new freight shed has been built at the Sehome Dock and other tracks are still going in for the convenience of the mill.

No accident to persons or property have been reported this year, although several cattle have been killed. Several miles of fence have been built and the damage is now much less from that cause. The line is now practically fenced where there is danger to stock, and the remaining fence will be completed next year. Already several applications for shingle mills, logging camps, and one lime works have been made on this new line.

Mr. Donovan's crews began steam shovel work in February, loading ballast for the line and sidetracks to be built for the accommodations of people in Everson and Sumas.

Future construction camps for the

SITE OF BELLINGHAM BAY AND BRITISH COLUMBIA BRIDGE CROSSING KENDALL CREEK
Originally at approximately 700 feet, the Kendall Creek Bridge was one of the longest on the Glacier Branch. It was a pile bent structure. (M. Impero)

MODIFIED KENDALL CREEK BRIDGE
Sometime in the 1950s or 1960s, the railroad company modified the bridge by filling most of it in with surplus rock from the limestone quarry. The whole wood structure is buried in this firm material and by walking on this grade railroad ties can be identified. (M. Impero)

surveyors would be located between the Herbert Leavitt and Hodge places, with their last camp being at Boulder Creek.

The clearing of ten miles from Sumas to Kendall Creek was completed. A large number of men then went to work on the next seven miles from Kendall Creek to Boulder Creek.

About ½ mile of track had been laid from Sumas, and eight miles of regrading was complete. It was expected to have the entire extension, seventeen miles in length, completed so that the trains could run over the road by Christmas.

The B. B. & B. C. track laying crew of 20 men completed the first two miles of the extension, reaching Lamberton

Station on the west side of Sumas River. After completing two bridges, they would work on a 90 foot one. Bridge number four, 4 miles out from Sumas and spanning the entrance to Saar Creek Canyon, was reached next. It would be the largest bridge of the 16 to be built on the line. At 70 feet high, 500 feet long, and with three decks, it would use 250,000 board feet of lumber and cost about $4000. Superintendent Donovan calculated that this bridge could be built in two weeks.

A gang of men was sent to Sumas to commence the construction of the foundation for a new eighty-ton track scale to be located near the junction of the mainline and its extension to Maple

Falls. Superintendent Donovan was on hand to supervise the commencement of the work. The scale was needed at this location due to all the freight being handled on the B. B. & B. C. line and the Canadian freight crossing the border.

The B. B. & B. C. reached a decision to extend their North Fork Line to the powerhouse at Nooksack Falls. On April 16, 1902, Engineer Warnick and his surveying party took to the field and began the actual line location. When the surveying work was complete, a bid call would be issued for the clearing and grubbing of that section. Donovan once again announced that Nelson and White of Seattle were awarded the contract to construct the Maple Falls to Glacier Creek Section, an estimated distance of ten miles. The contract called for doing the clearing, grubbing, grading,

riprap, and culvert work. Signed by Mr. Donovan, it involved about $100,000, or approximately $10,000 per mile. The contractor desired to place men on the entire length of the contract, subletting sections. The plan was to open a regular office locally. Nelson and White were building a warehouse/tool building in Maple Falls where they would have their headquarters. In the meantime, should contractors or men desire to communicate with them, they could be found at 201 Occidental Ave., Seattle. About ten carloads of supplies were shipped to Maple Falls and the work would be pushed to rapid completion. Very soon they would have 100 men engaged in the clearing and grubbing of the extension.

As per Donovan's instructions, the surveying of the route to Eastern Washington continued that summer.

TOWN OF KENDALL
Kendall sprang up after the arrival of the railroad in the Columbia Valley.
This community replaced the community of Keese. Kendall soon boasted a
post office, two stores, a town hall, a barbership, and a blacksmith shop.
(H. Johnson)

TOWN OF MAPLE FALLS

Maple Falls existed prior to the arrival of the railroad. With its arrival the small community really blossomed. The railroad provided transportation for all the timber products such as logs, sawn lumber, and shingles. The above picture was of Lake Street, which continued up Maple Creek Valley to Silver Lake. (E. Field)

The crew proceeded up the Nooksack River and upon reaching Ruth Creek continued up that drainage. Soon after reaching Hannegan Pass they continued over and down the Chilliwack River. Next came Indian Creek, over Whatcom Pass, and down Little Beaver Creek to the Skagit River. It is hard to determine upon reaching this point what course was taken as it is believed that the survey was discontinued at this point. The surveyor of the party reported to Donovan his findings and recommended that this route be abandoned. JJ then reported to San Francisco with his similar recommendation, and the matter was dropped.

On November 12, 1902, Donovan again requested sealed bids to be received until 1:00 p.m., Monday the 24th, for the construction of all pile trestles from the end of the track at Maple Falls to the Forest Reserve on the extension of the railroad. Each bid had to be accompanied by a certified check for $1500 payable to the B. B. & B. C. Company. The successful bidder was expected to begin work on December 1, 1902, and to execute the contract for the sum required. Failure to do so would require the loss of two surety bonds of $3000 each. Work had to be completed

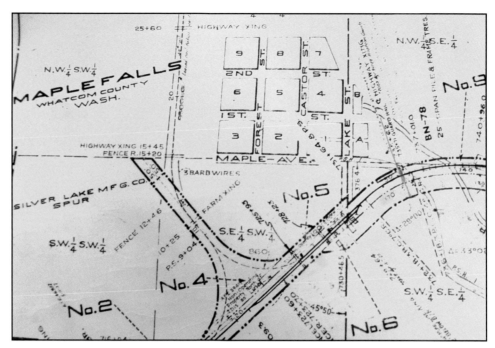

MAPLE FALLS AND THE BELLINGHAM BAY AND BRITISH COLUMBIA RAILROAD

The railroad entered the town in the lower left and made a sweeping turn to the right before continuing to Glacier. (Whatcom County Assessor)

by March 1, 1903. Further information would be found at the general office of the company in Whatcom, Washington. The right to reject any and all bids was reserved.

Materials for the construction of the line arrived on a daily basis. Two shipments of sixty-pound rail, the first being 500 tons, were shipped from New York on the steamer "California" and arrived at the Sehome Dock on December 1. The second cargo of 1000 tons would arrive at Sehome the following April 1. They would be sufficient for 17 miles of growth.

On March 11, 1903, construction on the B. B. & B. C. bridge to be built across the Nooksack at Steiner's was about to begin where Herman Steiner had homesteaded 160 acres of land.

A crew of men left the city for that purpose and George Scofied of Salvage and Scofied, who had the contract to build the bridge, left to supervise the work. He said that the work on the bridge would be started just as soon as the temporary bridge across Boulder Creek could be substituted by a new one, requiring three to four days. The work connected with the Nooksack Bridge would be difficult, he said, owing to the swift current of the river. Bulwarks of stone were built by the crew of men under the direction of Foreman Baxter. It would take about two months to complete the bridge.

In the fall of 1926, the Chicago, Milwaukee, and St. Paul Railroad, the future owners, would announce that they would be replacing the Nooksack

River Bridge at Warnick. A new bridge would be made necessary by the projected operation of two huge locomotives on the mainline. The present bridge would not be considered strong enough to bear the weight of the ordered engines. The stream would then be bridged by a 150-foot Howe truss span, with the timbers being framed at the company's Tacoma shops and creosoted before installation.

Rails were then laid on the B. B. & B. C. extension as far as Glacier Creek, where construction work for the year would end.

Donovan had requested and received a report that a survey from Goshen to Kendall had just been completed. This could modify the route to Glacier saving up to six miles; and JJ had workers standing ready to commence clearing the extension. The request was rejected by Cornwall in San Francisco.

Donovan's office had another bid call:

Bid call for the construction of a freight and passenger station 32' x 130' in size on Block 24, Lynden, for the Bellingham Bay and British Columbia Railroad Company will be received at my office in Whatcom until 2 p.m. on Saturday, November 7, 1903. The company will furnish all materials delivered on said block, excepting material for the concrete foundation blocks. Plans and specifications may be seen in my office, Whatcom, Washington. Each bid must be accompanied by a certified check of $100 payable to the B. B. & & B. C. Company. Which check will be forfeited unless contractor signs contract and furnishes bonds in the sum of $1000 for the complying with the terms of the

contract within ten days of award. The company reserves the right to reject any and all bids. JJ Donovan, General Superintendent.

The big news that the citizens of Glacier been waiting for came with a large crowd on hand at the Glacier Depot. The Bellingham Bay and British Columbia Railroad arrived in Glacier for the first time in January 1904.

Also in 1904, the Great Northern once again was rumored as a potential purchaser of the B. B. & B. C. Over the years it had been reported that several railroads had attempted to buy the company. General Superintendent Donovan flatly denied the report along with the others.

Sealed proposals will be received for clearing the right of way of the Bellingham Bay and British Columbia Railroad, 120 feet wide and seven miles in length, from Glacier eastward until 2:00 p.m., Wednesday, June 7, 1905. Specifications may be seen at the office of the company, Depot Building, Bellingham. Each bid must be accompanied by a certified check of $100 payable to the company as an evidence of good faith, which shall be forfeited if the successful bidder fails to execute the contract and security bond in the amount of $5000 within 15 days after the award of the contract. The right to reject any and all bids is reserved. JJ Donovan, General Superintendent, May 25, 1905.

There was no evidence found that this contract was ever awarded, and any work completed.

On March 31, 1906, JJ Donovan resigned his position. Following his resignation, he resumed his timber business interest with Julius Bloedel.

SITE OF A MAJOR NOOKSACK RIVER WASHOUT

One or two years following the completion of the railroad to Glacier, this was the site of a major river washout. Not previously having a complete knowledge of the Nooksack River, approximately 600 feet of track had to be replaced with a timber bulkhead for protection. (D. Jones)

NOOKSACK RIVER WASHOUT

It is believed that this photo and the previous one were taken from almost the same location. Apparently, it was shot at a later date as telephone poles can be seen alongside the tracks. The builders of the railroad put a lot of effort into this location to eliminate the possibility of a washout. To the right center is a bulkhead that was several hundred feet long that had been constructed to eliminate this issue. Unfortunately, it was not adequate. (W. Gannaway)

REMNANT OF THE WARNICK BRIDGE
Warnick was one of JJ's top surveyors and ran the line to Glacier and beyond. Upon crossing the river approximately four miles below Glacier, a timber trestle bridge was constructed. On the east side was the site of the Warnick Station located on the Steiner Homestead. The Warnick Lumber Mill was situated here as well. The only thing that remains of the bridge is this stone-built abutment on the west side. (M. Impero)

H. H. Taylor, recently appointed president, announced that Glen Hyatt was appointed manager and H. B. Paige, superintendent.

The Bellingham Bay and British Columbia planned to construct a new depot in Sumas to be located south of the United States Custom House. The old depot would be moved up the line and used as a freight house. The company was also planning to clean up and improve the depot grounds.

On July 31, 1908, the Bellingham Bay and British Columbia Railroad made an annual report of earnings and filed it with the State Tax Commissioner. This data indicated that gross earnings of the system for the past year, including freight and passengers, were $260,987.82. Total expenditures were $16,101.07. The road carried a total of 86,983 passengers, an average of 28.33 miles each, for which it received $62,972.17. Of the total freight tonnage, which amounted to 268,270 tons, 85,080 tons were lumber, while 154,645 tons were other forest products. The report shows that the road employed a total of 213 people, with an average daily wage of $2.48.

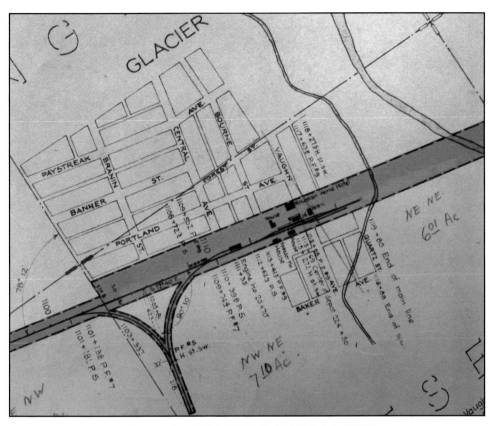

TOWN OF GLACIER RAILROAD SITE
The turnaround 'Y' can be easily seen and on close review all the buildings of the railroad, including the depot, can be located. Glacier was the end of the Sumas/Glacier run. (Whatcom County Assessor)

Glenn Hyatt, manager of the Bellingham Bay Improvement Company, and H. B. Paige, Superintendent of the Bellingham Bay and British Columbia Railroad, left for San Francisco to confer with President Taylor. While they were there, bids for the construction of the waterfront railroad line in Bellingham would be opened. On November 17, 1908, the City Council voted unanimously in favor of granting the waterfront franchise for a railroad to the Bellingham Bay and British Columbia Railroad. Protests came from eight to ten property owners, but the counsel ignored them, leaving such difficulties as may arise to be adjusted between "the property owners and the railroad company in court."

There were obvious reasons why the city approved the Great Northern and Bellingham Bay and British Columbia request for construction of waterfront tracks. The amount of downtown Bellingham train traffic was becoming unbearable and one of the worst offenders was the B. B. & B. C., particularly in the area of Railroad Avenue.

The two main reasons for the B. B. & B. C. making the request were

55

TOWN OF GLACIER
This picture is taken about the time the B. B. & B. C. arrived in Glacier. The packer on the right is a fellow by the name of Chet MacKenzie and it appears that he was heading out to the Lone Jack Mine or one of the other mines with supplies. Glacier, like Maple Falls, was a complete mountain town. However, with the arrival of the train rapid growth was known to the area. (Whatcom County Museum)

the fact that they were running out of space for car storage down at the end of Railroad Avenue, and that there was a very excessive grade about three miles north on the mainline coming out of the Squalicum Creek Bottom. In some cases, with a large load of logs on cars numbering up to 34, the assigned engine could not pull said grade and a second engine had to be connected to assist. The route that was to be used began at the point where the railroad crossed the current Hannegan Road and stayed on level ground, following Squalicum Creek to Bellingham Bay. It was a relatively easy road to make because the ground was relatively flat and only a few bridges needed to be constructed.

The Bellingham Bay Improvement

Company already owned a considerable amount of land on this proposed route, and the B. B. & B. C. easily acquired the remaining amount. Approximately halfway through the stretch of new track, a spur was made that went into the area that was later known as 'Marine Drive.' There they could provide service for the Olympic Portland Cement Company (O. P. C.), Oeser Cedar, and a sugar beet processing factory run by Utah-Idaho Sugar Beet Company.

This new rail section was operated by the newly incorporated entity called "Bellingham Terminal and Railroad Company." However, it was still under the total control of the B. B. & B. C.

In the summer of 1910, the word came that people of Whatcom County

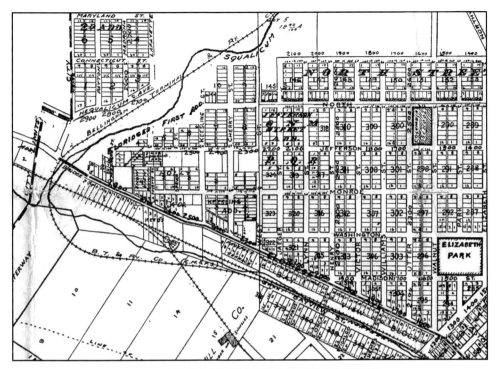

SQUALICUM CREEK BOTTOM ROUTE
The modified route was a major improvement to the B. B. & B. C. Railroad in many ways. (Whatcom County Assessor)

and the Bellingham Bay and British Columbia Railroad were waiting for. Construction on the lime plant near Kendall would begin soon. The work on a mile-long spur from the railroad mainline into the lime beds would be completed with the building of a trestle, and the factory near the Columbia Station would be under construction.

County Engineer Charles Lindbery and railroad engineers supervised the removal of a big log jam that threatened the railroad and the county bridge across the Nooksack River at Everson. The jam formed against the false work of the new railroad bridge during high water and had to be removed before another flood occurred.

From the Superintendent's Office of the B. B. & B. C.:

Dear Sir,

Referring to the violation of the 'Full Crew Bill' and the 'Federal Hours of Service Law': I am sending you the copies of two bulletins issued by Mr. Sawyer, Superintendent of the Bellingham Bay and British Columbia Railroad. There have been technical violations of the 'Full Crew Bill'. In two instances conductors on their own initiated and picked up enough train to make the four cars required in passenger trains to provide an extra brakeman.

I am convinced that certain newspapers here, owing to their love for you, will not understand the circumstances giving us credit for being honest in this investigation. I have promised both the newspapers that a

57

copy of my report will be sent to them from Olympia. Will you kindly see that this is done?

Bellingham Bay and British Columbia Railroad Company Office of the Superintendent, Bellingham, Washington, June 9, 1911

Bulletin #18:

Under the so-called 'Full Crew Law' which went into effect today, it is illegal for a freight train consisting of 25 or more cars to be operating without a conductor and three brakemen, or for a passenger train of four or more cars to be operating without a conductor and two brakemen.

It is the intention of the line to comply strictly with the terms of the law, but the conditions under which we are operating are such as it makes it impractical to have that maximum number of brakemen on each crew. The trainmaster will watch conditions closely, and in that endeavor, to so arrange the crews as to provide for prompt movement of all freight and for comfort accommodations for all passengers. Unusual and unforeseen conditions will arise from time to time, however, and the cooperation of the conductors will be necessary to avoid inconvenience to our patrons.

Freight conductors having two brakemen and finding more than 24 cars ready to move will at once communicate with the trainmaster. In the case it is impossible to reach him, conductors will use their judgment as to which cars to move in preference to which to leave. Passenger conductors with only one brakeman will not handle any more than three coaches. In the case more passengers appear and can be comfortably accommodated, the reason for the failure to provide additional equipment should be explained to them.

Bulletin #7: Train and Engine Men:

The attention of all concerned is directed to the 'Federal Hours of Service Law'. This provides, briefly, that train and engine men shall not be kept on duty longer than 16 hours; that having been on duty longer than 16 hours, they shall not resume duty without 10 hours of rest. The intention of this last clause being that they shall not be on duty more than 16 hours of any 24-hour period. It is the intention of the railroad to comply strictly with the terms of this law, and all employees will be expected to cooperate toward that end. It is believed that under normal conditions, a properly trained crew will be able to cover any of these runs in materially less than the 16-hour limit. Should a conductor find, however, that he will be longer than 16 hours to reach Bellingham, he will communicate with the trainmaster by any available means asking for instructions. Should he be unable to communicate with the train-master, it will set out whatever portions of the train is necessary to enable him to reach Bellingham within time.

There is an exemption from the operation of this line to cover the case of unavoidable and unforeseen accidents. Crews will not be expected or permitted to tie up when the mainline is blocked, without special instructions from the trainmaster or myself.

Signed,
Mott Sawyer

In the summer of 1911, the Public Service Commission of Washington came forward to do an inspection of the Bellingham Bay and British Columbia Railroad. It is not known if this was simply routine or was brought about by concerned citizens.

At some point the Bellingham Herald joined in on the inspection. The first item in this report was a letter from H. A. Fairchild, Chairman of the Commission, which was written to the Herald.

Dear Sir:

In accordance with our Mr. Perley statement to you, we enclose here a copy of his report made to this commission, and that fullest publicity may be given, we also enclose copies of letters of transaction.

We will simply add that Mr. Perley was instructed to make a thorough investigation of these lines, and if the conditions of the track justified, to exercise the power confirmed to him of suspending train operations or limiting the speed over any defective part of the track.

In a formal communication to this commission Mr. Perley stated that assurances were given him that the track through the swamp on the Lynden Branch referred to would be raised and improved at once.

The commission will continue to endeavor to discharge its duty to the public, respective to criticism and uninfluenced by the hopes of compensation.

Very truly yours,
The Public Service Commission of Washington, H. A. Fairchild, Chairman.

The Report:
Gentleman: On my arrival here

Monday to investigate the track conditions on the Bellingham Bay and British Columbia Railroad, I found the impression had been given out that any investigation by The Public Service Commission would be somewhat superficial and biased. Before meeting any of the officers of the railroad company, I called on both newspaper companies and told them I intended to walk over the Lynden Branch on Tuesday morning and invited them to send representatives with me. I did this to convince the public that the condition of the track on this line would be truthfully reported. I then called Mr. Sawyer, the superintendent, and told him of my intention, and that I should be pleased to have someone representing the railroad company accompany me on this inspection. On Tuesday morning, accompanied by Mr. Sawyer, Superintendent of the Line, Mr. Naff representing the press, and Mr. Gilroy, Road Manager, we walked from Lynden to the Hampton Junction, approximately five miles.

The Lynden branch has been built about eight years. The line is straight with the exception of one curve near Hampton Junction of 4°. It is laid with fifty-pound steel rails, 4-inch steel base, English make, that, owing to past service, is quite badly surfaced bent, rendering it impossible to use to make a smooth track. The ties, except for about 1 mile through a low swampy area, are good. Five hundred and nine bad ties in this swamp were found on the branch, all of them within a distance of about 1½ miles. The rails through this swamp 'have run,' and those ties that were spiked through the slot in the angle bars have been moved out of place, and this won't 'have run,' and affecting your regular spacing of the ties, and making the track look worse than it really is. The track at this point is low and is at times covered with water. A few joints were noted with a bolt missing. Apart from the surface bending of the rails, and they are in good condition, the ball of the rail and the ends are not battered. The track is a good gauge. While considering whether the track is safe or unsafe for the operation, the character in the volume of traffic must be taken into consideration. Many miles of railroad in the state would not be safe for the operation of transcontinental trains at their regular speed but might be perfectly safe for the work required to be done over them. In the case of the Lynden Branch, it ought to have about 400 new ties put in on the mile and a half of the track referred to above in order to make that portion correspond with the rest of the line. With the present speed regulations on this line, I consider it quite safe to operate. Engines weighing 65 to 85 tons are used in freight service making one trip for the line each day. With the light rail and narrow rail base it would be necessary to insist on speed regulations which the company has done. I have also been over the mainline of the Bellingham Bay and British Columbia Railroad from Bellingham to Glacier. This portion of the line is equipped with sixty-pound steel rails from Bellingham to Sumas, fifty-six-pound rails from Sumas to Maple Falls and sixty-pound rails from Maple Falls to Glacier. The track is in good condition. Employees who have been in the service of the company before the construction of the Lynden branch tell me that there had never been a derailment on that portion of the line, except in the yard of Lynden while staking cars, and in one instance the engine ran off the end of the switch. On the 48 miles of line there are 56 section men employed, including eight foremen.

Bellingham, Washington, August 16, 1911

Hon. Fairchild, Chairman Public Service Commission, Olympia, Washington

A large expansion was constructed in the summer of 1915 by the Bellingham and Northern Railroad. (Now a subsidiary of the Chicago, Milwaukee, and St. Paul Railroad, or simply, the 'Milwaukee', that purchased the B. B. & B. C. around this time. See Chapter 10.) This branch of the railroad was identified as the Goshen-Kulshan Line. The main purpose for this construction project was to open up the Middle Fork Drainage of the Nooksack River to train services.

Up until this point, this region had not had any major logging operations. With the advent of the railroad a vast amount of timberland was made available.

The St. Paul and Tacoma Lumber Company, one of the largest timber/lumber concerns in the Pacific Northwest, mainly in the southern part of the state, had acquired the majority of the timberlands of this valley. This operation would become known as the St. Paul and Tacoma Lumber Company, Nooksack Camp.

The line would branch off the mainline at Goshen and contour basically on level land around to an area identified as Kulshan.

By June 1, 1915, the construction

of the Goshen-Kulshan Branch of the Milwaukee was progressing at a record pace. A crew of 250 workers were working around the clock and reports stated that the entire right of way for twelve miles had been cleared with the exception of 3000 feet, located where the company was having some trouble getting the right of way. Three miles had been graded.

On July 19, 1915, news was released concerning the biggest projects in the construction of the Goshen-Kulshan Railroad Branch - the construction of two bridges across the Nooksack.

The first was at a crossing at the end of the Smith Road. The river at this point included all three forks. The next bridge was to be constructed just above the confluence of the Middle Fork and the North Fork. A large bridge building crew of between 25 and 30 men, in the employment of the Chicago, Milwaukee, and St. Paul Railroad, arrived in Bellingham on its way to Goshen where it would prepare the timbers, rods, etc., for the two Howe truss bridges. It was estimated that about a month would be required for the preliminary work. The bridges would be

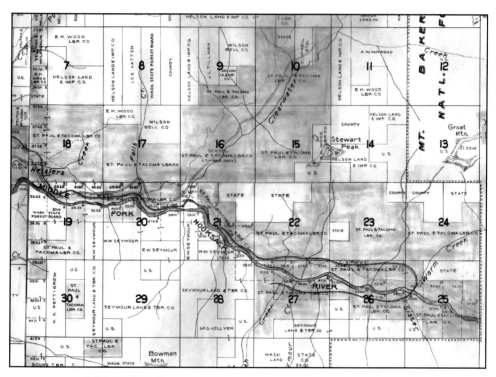

PORTION OF TIMBER OWNED BY ST. PAUL AND TACOMA LUMBER COMPANY

This map illustrates in yellow the land holdings of the St. Paul and Tacoma Lumber Company. It would have taken four different maps to show the vast timberlands (15,000 acres) that the company owned up the Middle Fork of the Nooksack River. An example is the 640 acres of surveyed land in section number 16. This was one of the largest operations on different private lands within Whatcom County. (G. Raper)

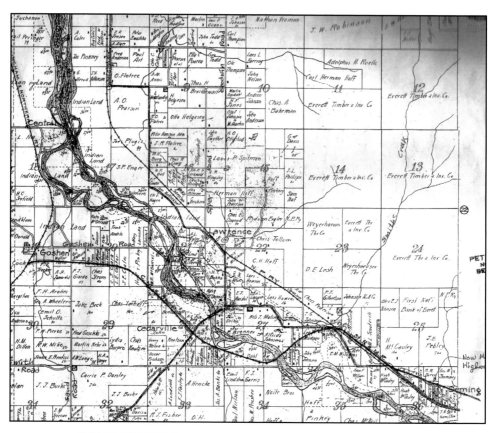

GOSHEN/KULSHAN BRANCH OFF THE MAINLINE
The Goshen/Kulshan Branch followed a relatively flat route to Canyon Creek.
It required construction of two major covered bridges across the Nooksack
River. (G. Raper)

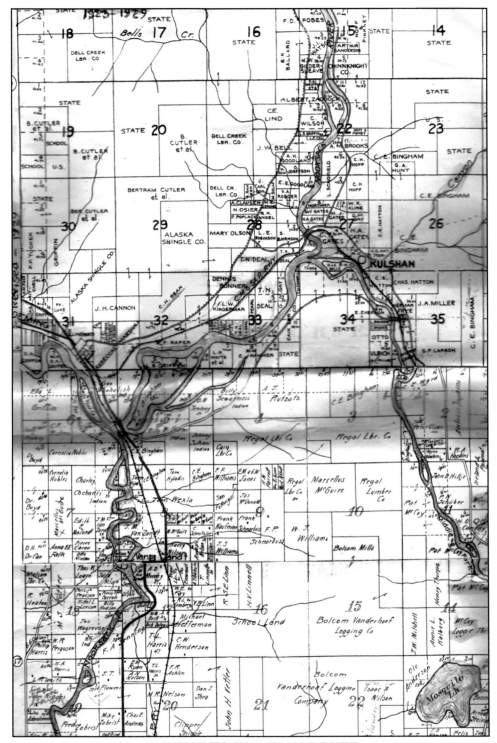

DEMING TO KULSHAN ROUTE
This is a continuation of the previous page and shows the road to its end at
Canyon Creek. (G. Raper)

COVERED BRIDGE OF THE NOOKSACK

The Chicago, Milwaukee, and St. Paul Railroad constructed two covered bridges to cross the Nooksack River, the first being in the vicinity of the east end of the Smith Road. The one pictured above spanned the North Fork, one of three forks. The author is not aware of any other covered railroad bridges in Whatcom County. (G. Raper)

GOSHEN-KULSHAN BRANCH BRIDGE RIVER VIEW

As mentioned, the Goshen-Kulshan Branch of the Milwaukee crossed the Nooksack River in two different locations: first, near the end of the present Smith Road, and second, near the convergence of the North and Middle Forks. The two were covered bridges to protect them from the weather. It is not known if they were originally built that way. (Whatcom County Museum)

REVIEWING BRIDGE DAMAGE
An engineer is inspecting the deteriorating condition of the Welcome Bridge.
It was originally used by the railroad; but with the shutdown of that use, it
became a logging truck bridge. Following that, all county road traffic crossed
it while a new county bridge was being built. (Whatcom County Museum)

built by the local railroad itself and
the arriving crew would have with
it seven cars with supplies, lodging
quarters, etc.

With a larger crew of about 40
men, Dan Crowley, one of the oldest
and best known bridge builders on
the Pacific Coast, began the framing
of timbers and other work that was
preliminary to the construction of

the two Howe truss bridges. In addition
to these, four other bridges would
be built and it was estimated that six
months would be required to complete
them all. The bridge crew would spend
several weeks doing the preliminaries
at a camp that had been established at
Goshen. Crowley had been building
bridges in the Northwest for 35 years.

It was estimated that approximately

75% of the grading was complete on the Goshen-Welcome Branch of the Milwaukee; and the entire roadbed would be ready for rails in three or four months, according to Arthur Sullivan, who had general charge of the work for Twohy Brothers Construction Company. The work would have been further advanced but for changes made in the right of way several weeks before. Practically all the light part of the improvement was finished, but there remained several rock cuts and about half of a 200-foot tunnel. Construction of some of the small bridges which Twohy Brothers would build were started. Again, the large bridges would be built by the Chicago, Milwaukee, and St. Paul Railroad by a crew at

Goshen who created the bridge timbers and assembled all materials so that the structure could be put together quickly.

The work of laying the rail on the Goshen-Kulshan Branch began and four miles were laid to the first crossing of the Nooksack. Following that, track construction would continue to Welcome. The plans of the engineer in charge of the extension, James Wilson, provided for the completion of the remaining twelve miles of road by May 1916. Work along the line progressed so well that relatively little remained to be done, aside from cutting through the rocky obstructions near Deming.

After crossing the Nooksack River at Welcome, the Goshen/Kulshan Branch went up the Middle Fork to

THE MILWAUKEE RAILROAD APPROACHING THE MUD CUT
This 1920 photo shows from left to right the following: Goshen-Kulshan Branch, Mount Baker Highway, Northern Pacific Railway, and the Nooksack River. To the left of the railroad is a year-round pond. When the railroad was abandoned, it became the roadbed for the current Mount Baker Highway. The roadway in the middle of the picture is almost totally abandoned today. (Deming Library)

ONLY TUNNEL OF THE MILWAUKEE LINE

This 200-foot tunnel was located on what is currently the Mount Baker Highway, approximately half a mile beyond Deming where the highway cuts through solid rock near a year-round pond. Eventually the State Highway Department took over the right of way to make it into part of the Mount Baker Highway. (Deming Library)

MAJOR ROCK CUT

This rock cut was in the immediate area of the rock tunnel. In the construction of the Goshen-Kulshan Branch little rock excavation was required. (D. Jones)

ST. PAUL AND TACOMA LUMBER COMPANY - NOOKSACK CAMP #7
The St. Paul and Tacoma Company - Nooksack Camp #7 was one of the
largest and most modern in Whatcom County. (Whatcom County Museum)

Canyon Creek. That was the end of rail for the Chicago, Milwaukee, and St. Paul Railroad, and where Hoff and Pinky located a large sawmill. Along the line there were numerous logging and milling operations and at this point three independent logging companies continued their own lines. They were Boone & Company, Buffelin Lumber Company, and St. Paul and Tacoma Lumber Company, the largest. Camp #7 opened in the summer of 1923.

The Goshen/Kulshan Branch was abandoned in 1943.

The Lake Whatcom Branch was the last constructed (1916) by the Chicago, Milwaukee, and St. Paul Railroad in Whatcom County. The railroad provided service to the Bloedel Donovan Larson Mill (1901-1946) located on the northwest end of Lake Whatcom.

The new road branched off the original Bellingham rail line, turning in an easterly direction one block north of Oregon Street and crossing the Northern Pacific grade. It next crossed the west side of Alabama Hill and entered what is now Whatcom Falls Park on a wide turn. Finally, a high trestle bridged Whatcom Creek before the tracks entered the mill yard. The main usage of the line was to haul the company's finished products for distribution to various parts of the world.

It provided service until the mill completely burned.

ST. PAUL AND TACOMA COOKHOUSE AND DINING ROOM
Cookhouse and dining room with full staff. (Whatcom County Museum)

ST. PAUL AND TACOMA DINING ROOM
In logging camps, it was not the wages that kept the good loggers, but the quality and quantity of the food. At mealtime all the loggers were served at one time, in this case between 200 and 300 meals. (Whatcom County Museum)

BLOEDEL DONOVAN AND LARSON MILL
Bloedel Donovan and Larson was the largest logging and lumber milling
business in the Pacific Northwest. The mill operated for many years on Lake
Whatcom and completely logged off all the timber from both sides of the lake
down to Park at the south end. Following that they then started down on the
South Fork drainage around Saxon. (D. Jones)

NORTHERN PACIFIC LOG SPILL

Both the Chicago, Milwaukee, and St. Paul Railroad and Northern Pacific
Railroad traversed Alabama Hill in Bellingham to get to the Larson Mill on
Lake Whatcom. The Northern Pacific crossed Alabama Street by means of a
constructed trestle and the Milwaukee crossed on-grade below it. If Alabama
Street at that time would have been as wide as it is today, some of the logs
probably would have rolled all the way to the bottom. (Whatcom County
Museum)

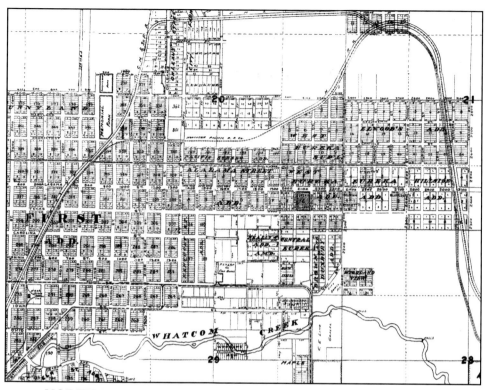

NORTHERN PACIFIC AND MILWAUKEE PARALLEL LINES
The Northern Pacific was first to reach the mill on Lake Whatcom. The line continued down the north side to the Blue Canyon Coal Company and then south, directly into Skagit County. (Whatcom County Assessor)

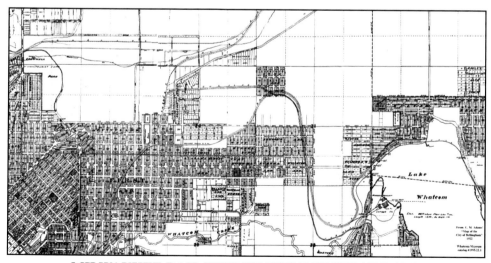

MILWAUKEE RAIL TERMINATION POINT AT LAKE
Upon reaching flat land at the top of Alabama Hill, the railroad made a sweeping turn over Whatcom Creek and directly into the mill site. To cross, a very elaborate high trestle was constructed. (Whatcom County Assessor)

WHATCOM CREEK HIGH TRESTLE
While the ends of the trestle have collapsed, visitors can still view the middle section from trails in Whatcom Falls Park. (M. Impero)

PROFILE CHART OF THE B. B. & B. C. RAILROAD GRADE

The railroad grade for the mainline and all branches is shown. (W. Gannaway)

75

Chapter 4
Construction of Spurs

The construction of railroad spurs varied significantly depending on who owned the spur and who constructed it. Other factors were how long was the spur to be used, and was it going to be used year-round or only in the summer? Also, how heavy were the loads to be and at what speed was the train expected to travel?

If the spurs were to be constructed by companies like the Bellingham Bay and British Columbia Railroad, they were normally built to high standards, even though it might not match the quality of the mainline run. Many factors determined quality, such as rail condition, rail weight, drainage on both sides of the rail bed, and the quality of bridges and trestles. Many logging spurs were constructed, and in most cases, were only good enough to get by for a short period of time before being abandoned.

It is extremely difficult in reviewing all the available information to determine the ownership of many of these spurs. Who did the clearing and grubbing? Who furnished and installed the rail? Who furnished and installed the ballast? In some cases, the costs

EXAMPLE OF ADEQUATE SPUR CONSTRUCTION
This example is sufficient for one summer of use. Note, there is no drainage on the uphill side, and it appears in some spots that the cut of the bank is too steep and bank caving will occur. (D. Jones)

EXAMPLE OF A TERRIBLE SPUR ROAD
This spur line represents a derailment about to happen. It appears that the ties are placed directly on natural earth of some sort. There is no ballast, no drainage, and the rails are not laid straight. (D. Jones)

that occurred for spur construction amounted to a great deal of money, such as the Chinn Spur.

According to Kramer Adams's book, *Logging Railroads of the West*, there existed, or had existed, 46 railroad logging companies in Whatcom County through the 1950s.

CAMPBELL TIMBER COMPANY SPUR

The Campbell Timber Company Spur was the most unique one created by the B. B. & B. C. Railroad. On this spur the railroad crossed the international border into Canada.

Campbell Timber Company had vast timber holdings around Cultus Lake and up on the surrounding mountains, such as Vedder Mountain in Canada. This remote area is due south of the Canadian city of Chilliwack. At the time of Campbell Timber, there was no nearby train system access to the lake area.

H. W. Hunter, president of the Campbell River Lumber Company, Ltd. of White Rock, B. C. and mayor of Blaine, was in Bellingham when he

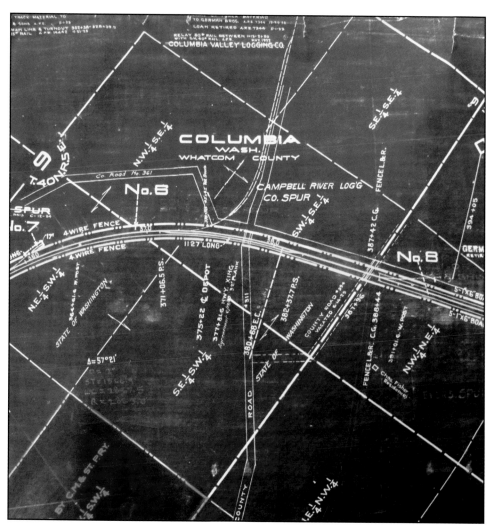

CAMPBELL TIMBER COMPANY SPUR
The location of the spur branching off the mainline is illustrated in this map. The spur connection is almost in the center of the picture and is heading in an easterly direction toward Silver Lake. (Whatcom County Assessor)

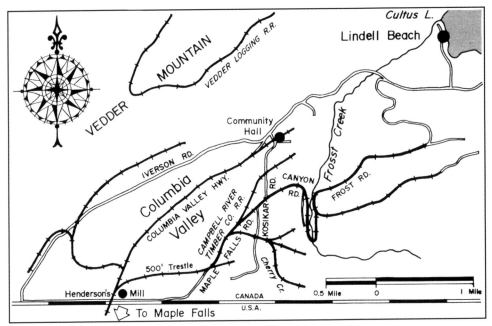

COLUMBIA VALLEY IN BRITISH COLUMBIA

The above map shows the area from the border to Cultus Lake which was mainly controlled by the Campbell Timber Company. At the bottom left is an arrow indicating the direction to Maple Falls. However, at this point the railroad turned to the left and headed west toward the Columbia Depot. (*The Fraser Valley Challenge*, p. 88)

CAMPBELL TIMBER COMPANY UNITED STATES SPUR

This roadbed would have been constructed somewhere between the quality of the mainline and a spur. This spur was used for a long duration and had to withstand the heavy traffic of hauling many logs. The location of this picture is directly behind the original site of the Silver Lake School. (M. Impero)

announced arranging for steel rail for the railroad his company would build to tap 9000 acres of timber it recently purchased between the boundary line and Cultus Lake. Approximately six miles of railroad would be built to the border from Columbia, a station on the Milwaukee Line (formerly the B. B. & B. C.) southwest of Kendall. Log hauling would be started in time to ship out more than 1,500,000 board feet by December 1, 1922. Daily shipments to Bellingham would be about 25 cars after the camp began capacity operation. The cedar on the track, representing about 15% of the whole area, would be cut into shingles, making it necessary to build a shingle mill at the site.

Permission for crossing the border was granted from both countries. This spur turned off the Sumas to Glacier Run at the Columbia Station and continued up the valley in an easterly direction toward Silver Lake. Approaching the Silver Lake School, the route turned behind the school and proceeded into Canada, operating for many years. However, at some point in time Chilliwack and the surrounding area received their own railroad line.

CHINN-KNIGHT SPUR

Raleigh Chinn was one of many that were waiting for the B. B. & B. C. Railroad to arrive in the upper Nooksack Valley. He was a successful timber man in the southern part of the state and had heard of the great timberlands of the Nooksack Valley. With the arrival of the train he jumped at the opportunity to move north.

His chosen area was on a mountain across the river from the town of Maple Falls. Slide Mountain was named after

a slide occurred in about 1900 on its north end. This was a vast amount of timberland starting at the river and continuing uphill to the crest of the mountain at an elevation of about 3200 feet. The timberlands started north of the slide and continued south to Racehorse Creek.

Like many other prosperous timber men, he arrived in the area and started buying up timberland homesteading claims on Slide Mountain. They ranged in different sizes, but normally were 160 acres. The bulk of all these claims had been proven up by the homesteaders and ownership was clear. These homesteaders had no intention of living on them permanently and had only proven them up for the fact that they intended to sell to timber barons in the future.

As soon as the railroad arrived in Maple Falls, Chinn had prepared an application for a spur which was to cross the Nooksack River. It was granted. His intended spur was to run southeast of the mainline and hit the river at Chinn Canyon. The first bridge built across the Nooksack at this location was a pile bent structure which washed out in a few years. A clear span bridge was then built. These bridges were approximately 592 feet long.

Once across the river on basically level ground, Chinn made his first camp. He later made a second camp at the top of a 46° railroad incline. Each could accommodate 200 men. At the lower one where families were living in crude shacks, Chinn established a school in 1903 that became part of the Washington State School District #80. R. E. Chinn was the director and clerk. Twelve pupils attended the three-

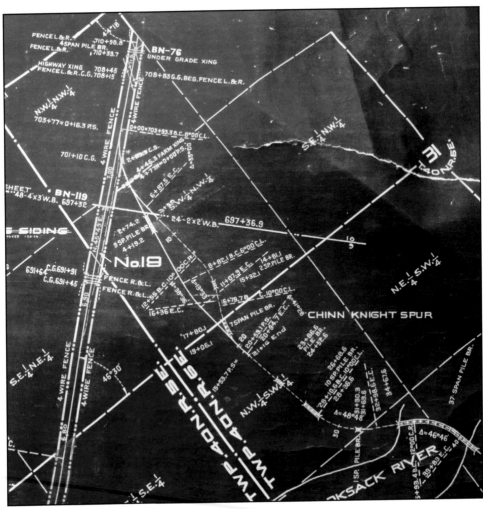

MAPLE FALLS CHINN-KNIGHT SPUR

Chinn-Knight Spur branched off the mainline a short distance southwest of
Maple Falls. The distance of this spur was approximately 4165 feet, and upon
crossing the Nooksack River it stopped. It was put in with major expense and
how that expense was divided between the railroad and the timber company
is not known. Three bridges were built from Maple Falls where a massive one
was constructed with a length of approximately 592 feet on the curve crossing
the river. This bridge later washed out and was replaced with a span bridge.
(Whatcom County Assessor)

CHINN-KNIGHT TRAIN LOGGING
In the early days of logging on Slide Mountain where the land was relatively flat, the logging was performed by a locomotive. In this picture the logs are being dragged on a skid bed between the rails. This process was used for a short period of time and then replaced with high lead yarding of the logs. (Whatcom County Museum)

month term, housed in a one room camp building. It ran for years until the children were eventually transported to the Maple Falls School.

In the early 1900s the Chinn Timber Company was often referred to as the death camp since it had an exceptionally high number of logging fatalities. In some cases, following a death they would just go back to work, not even stopping for the day.

Over a period of approximately 25 years, like all other timber companies, the camp had economic good times and bad times. Just prior to the Great Depression, the Chinn Company went broke in 1928.

CHINN-KNIGHT RAILROAD INCLINE

Chinn-Knight exclusively used railroads for moving the logs. They constructed a whole series of railroad grades with trestles across the face of Slide Mountain. Later, to get the logs down more efficiently to the lower level for shipment by the B. B. & B. C. Railroad, a two-mile railroad incline was built going directly downhill at a 46° angle. A large snubbing machine was located at the top of the hill for lowering the cars of logs and pulling up the empties. This system operated 1903-1928. (Whatcom County Museum)

LIMESTONE SPUR

With limestone discovered up in Columbia Valley, Whatcom County, an enormous surge in business was created. The B. B. & B. C. Railroad was one of the local businesses with the most interest because the railroad was going to run directly through the center of Columbia Valley and this limestone deposit would become a very valued customer.

The limestone was found approximately two to three miles north of Kendall and located on both Sumas Mountain and Red Mountain. With little investigation and site work, it was determined that this deposit was of an extremely high grade and had a tremendous quantity of future rock.

The first operation to be developed by The International Lime Company was at the base of Red Mountain. This company's main functions were the mining of the ore, processing it into lime, bagging it, and finally, shipping it throughout the Northwest by way of the Bellingham Bay and British Columbia Railroad.

The issue of land ownership of two distinctly different parcels of land

OLYMPIC PORTLAND CEMENT BELLINGHAM PLANT
The Bellingham cement plant was located northwest of the city on Marine Drive, or Northwest Diagonal Road. It was on a high bench of land overlooking Bellingham Bay in the direction toward the entrance of the Nooksack River. Marine Drive is the diagonal road in the lower right corner of the picture and crossing it at an approximate 90° angle is a spur of the Bellingham Bay and British Columbia Railroad. This was an ideal location for the plant because of the availability of two railroads and deep water to construct a pier for water shipment. Look and see how few houses were around the plant and then think of it today. (I. Olson, Lehigh Cement Group)

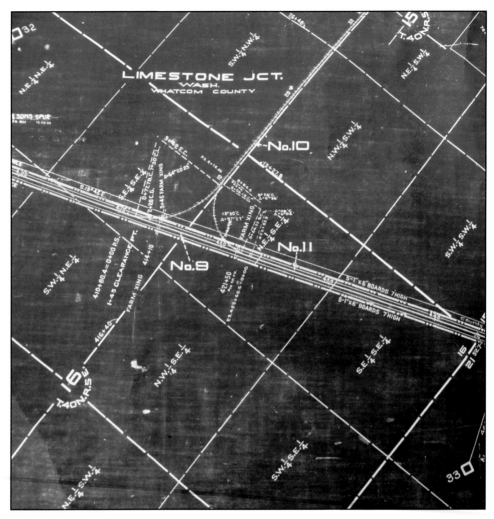

RED MOUNTAIN LIMESTONE SPUR

The Olympic Portland Cement Spur is shown as "No. 10." Note that there is a 'Y' at the intersection with the main B. B. & B. C. Railroad. This would allow trains to go up or down the mainline with the locomotive in the head position. On the following page "No. 10" can be followed to the base of the hill and the operation. This was the site of the original International Lime Company and the final location for the O. P. C. operation. (Whatcom County Assessor)

with the limestone deposit became a heated battle. This real estate conflict was finally processed all the way to the Ninth Circuit Court of Appeals. It became so complex and hard to understand that the final court determination is not known. What is known is that this ownership dispute did not affect The International Lime Company.

Once the ownership was decided, the Olympic Portland Cement Company (O. P. C.) was formed and became the operating company. The first of the two

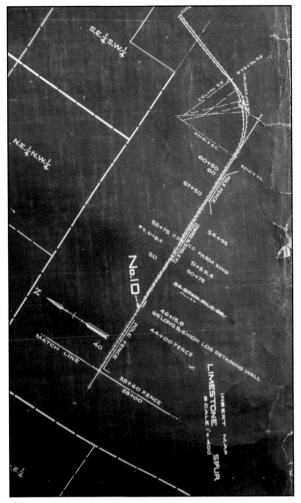

EAST END OF LIMESTONE JUNCTON SPUR
At the curve near the end was the site of the International Lime Company and future O. P. C. Red Mountain Operation. (Whatcom County Assessor)

locations that were to operate under O. P. C.'s direction was on the Sumas Mountain side of the valley.

With the spur created by the B. B. & B. C. and with land clearing, the site was quickly developed. Four distinctly different quarry sites were put into production, along with full crushing equipment, storage, and railroad loading facilities.

Balfour, the O. P. C. "Company Town," was developed at the site. Twelve family cottages were constructed for the married workers with families. A large bunkhouse with cookhouse was erected and served as a community service building, used for meetings, church services, and boxing matches. The town also had an additional number of small cabins that were used by the unmarried workers. With a baseball diamond providing the field, Balfour had a company team that competed with high school teams, other

87

THE INTERNATIONAL LIME COMPANY

This company came into the valley, procured some open land with high-quality limestone, and started the plant. The process was to mine the limestone at the top of the mountain, bring it down to the plant by tramway buckets, and then produce it into lime. It was then shipped out in bags by the B. B. & B. C. Railroad to be used up and down the Pacific Coast. This operation started in 1909 or 1910 and closed on September 14, 1926. The plant was dismantled and reinstalled down in Oregon for the Black Marble and Lime Company. The Olympic Portland Cement Company then purchased the land and operated at this site in Whatcom County for many years. (I. Olson, Lehigh Cement Group)

RED MOUNTAIN OLYMPIC PORTLAND CEMENT TRAMWAY SYSTEM
In the beginning of the limestone discovery in Columbia Valley, many of the disputed companies were planning to build a cement plant at the site; and the International Lime Company did process the limestone rock into lime there. However, the Olympic Portland Cement Company was totally different in that their whole process was to mine and transport the limestone down the hillside by tramway. The processing of cement was moved completely to Bellingham. For years the limestone rock was shipped by the Bellingham Bay and British Columbia Railroad and the Chicago, Milwaukee, and St. Paul Railroad. Following the closure of the tracks it was trucked to Bellingham by Lynden Transport Company. (I. Olson, Lehigh Cement Group)

OLYMPIC PORTLAND CEMENT COMPANY LTD., ENGINE NO. 2
The Olympic Portland Cement Company had two of these locomotives. One was used at the plant site in Bellingham, and the other was used up at the quarries in Columbia Valley. The one in Bellingham was displayed for years at Bloedel Donovan Park. (I. Olson, Lehigh Cement Group)

O. P. C. RED MOUNTAIN QUARRY
This quarry was opened and mining began in 1929. Operations continued until the late 1970s. The quantity and quality have varied over the years, but the mountain is still full of limestone. (I. Olson, Lehigh Cement Group)

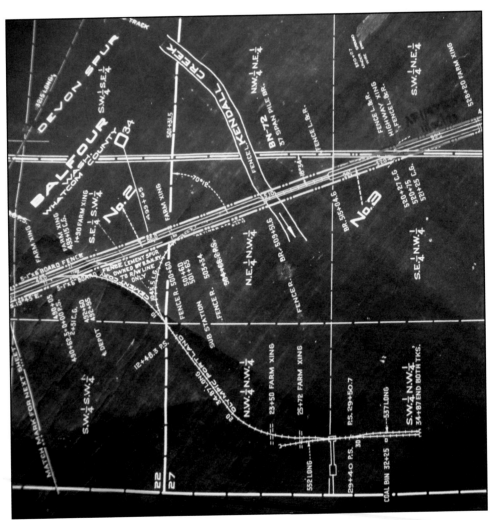

SUMAS MOUNTAIN WEST SPUR IN COLUMBIA VALLEY
The spur left the mainline at the Balfour Depot and was a total of 3487 feet long. This operation was similar to the O. P. C. operation across the valley in mining and shipping out limestone rock. The crusher here was not actually a crusher but a rock chipper. (Whatcom County Assessor)

TOWN OF BALFOUR

The company town of Balfour was on the west side of the valley and was the first area that the Olympic Portland Cement Company mined. You can see the width of Columbia Valley and near the top of the photo on the opposite hillside is the second O. P. C. Quarry operation. The married men cottages are seen; and the two-story building, lower center of the photo, is the bunkhouse, cookhouse, and meeting hall. The open field to the left is the baseball diamond. (I. Olson, Lehigh Cement Group)

MARRIED MEN COTTAGES

These cabins were laid out very neatly and were comfortable to live in with linoleum floors and oil heaters. In the street between the rows there were fire hydrants. The railroad and automobile roads ran parallels through the property. (I. Olson, Lehigh Cement Group)

COOKHOUSE, BUNKHOUSE, AND ASSEMBLY HALL

This was the "Company Town" multi-use building for weddings to birthdays and everything in between. By looking closely one can see on the wall a display of Darius Kinsey photographs. Kinsey, a very noted photographer, would travel throughout the Northwest taking pictures and then returning to the site to sell them. His main clientele was logging camps; however, one can see that he also did other kinds of operations. He would travel by train and later by automobile. (I. Olson, Lehigh Cement Group)

company teams, and the team from the Civilian Conservation Corps Camp at Glacier.

ALLEN-MCREA LOGGING SPUR

Allen-McRea was a successful logging company in the upper Nooksack River Region. In 1900 the Forest Service opened timberlands for logging. One of the first timber sales sold was above Glacier and Allen-McRea was the successful bidder. The first item of business was connecting with the B. B. & B. C. at the end of the line in Glacier and building the railroad to the site. The actual timber sale was on the opposite side of the Nooksack River so a bridge crossing it became necessary. Additionally, bridges had to be built across Glacier Creek and Gallup Creek.

The greatest challenge of building this line was to construct that bridge across the Nooksack River at a location almost exactly where the Douglas Fir Campground is situated today.

ALLEN-MCREA LOGGING CAMP
The first items of business were the construction of the railroad and the logging camp. Church Mountain is visible in the upper left part of the picture with Excelsior Ridge to its right. (Whatcom County Museum)

ALLEN-MCREA NORTH FORK NOOKSACK BRIDGE

This bridge is unique and shows the skill of railroad builders without any formal education. The section to the right is on high terrain and to the left it is not as high in elevation. Thus, this bridge had to be built up on cribs. The actual flow of the river is to the right of the picture and the total length of the structure is unknown. Special attention is drawn to the railroad ties which appear in some cases to be just small, round trees. Also note about this bridge, all the logs that are shown in its construction were put into place without any fasteners of any kind. Upon demolition this allowed the logs to be shipped to a mill and the lumber cut without hitting bolts or nails. (Whatcom County Museum)

EXAMPLE OF HIGH-LEVEL ENGINEERING
This marvel of engineering was probably created on a big scale logging operation which had its own logging engineer. The bridge could have been something that JJ Donovan would have designed. The accepted span for this type of bridge would be a maximum length of between 80 and 90 feet. After the first bent bridge at Chinn Canyon was washed away, this probably would have been the type of bridge that replaced it. (G. Tweit)

FRED FOBES-MAPLE FALLS/ SILVER LAKE SPUR

Fred Fobes was a highly successful businessman in Washington State. His main business location was in Seattle; however, his main timber holdings were up in Whatcom County around Warnick, Wickersham, Glacier, and Maple Falls. One of his main areas was the Maple Creek Valley from Maple Falls to Silver Lake. In addition, he had many partnerships with other logging companies that were constantly changing.

The B. B. & B. C. built a spur that left the mainline west of Maple Falls behind the Maple Falls School site, and then continued up the Maple Creek Valley, eventually continuing with tracks on both sides of Silver Lake.

He constructed two different mills on Maple Creek on land which was later to become the Patsy Impero Farm (author's grandfather). The first was a shingle mill, followed by a large sawmill. Both burned down in about 1926.

When the logging played out, Fobes cleaned up the whole area and made it into a beautiful farm. He built a handsome home with a caretaker house at the north end of the former mill pond. It was referred to as the 'Fobes Mansion.'

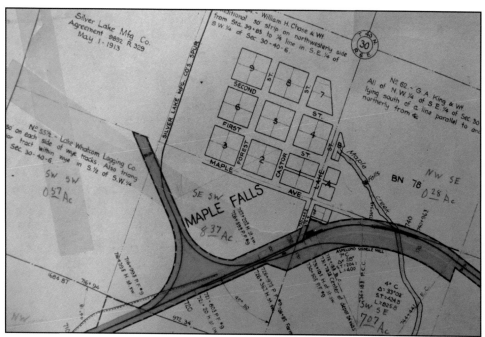

FOBES/SILVER LAKE MANUFACTURING COMPANY SPUR
The Fobes/Silver Lake Manufacturing Company Spur intersected the
B. B. & B. C. at the west end of Maple Falls. This photo shows the platted
town. (Whatcom County Assessor)

SILVER LAKE SHINGLE COMPANY
The Silver Lake Shingle Company was situated approximately two miles
north of Maple Falls on Maple Creek. This mill was destroyed by fire and then
replaced with a sawmill by the name of Silver Lake Manufacturing Company,
mainly owned by Fred Fobes. (M. Impero)

**B. B. & B. C. ENGINE #2
NAMEPLATE**
Heidi Doornenbal is the
current owner of the farm
that was created by Fred
Fobes and Patsy Impero. Her
home and farm buildings set
approximately where the Silver
Lake Shingle Mill Company
and Silver Lake Manufacturing
Company were located. While
digging a hole this nameplate
was discovered. With a
thorough cleaning it was found
to be from B. B. & B. C. Engine
#2. They thought that possibly
the whole engine was in this
area and so continued to dig.
Nothing further was found.
(M. Impero)

Following his timber ventures, Fobes then entered into the field of electrical supply. In the Seattle area he built warehouses and distribution points for all types of electrical equipment.

Fred Fobes was a very friendly and likable man in the little community of Maple Falls, serving on the Maple Falls School Board and the Maple Falls Council. He would catch the train out of Seattle to Maple Falls just to attend those meetings.

MOGUL-TRAMWAY SPUR

Mogul-Tramway Spur was located northwest and southwest of Clearbrook. The spur was in the vicinity of Judson Lake and Pangborn Lake, almost at the Canadian border. In this area the land was extremely swampy with standing water, and it was difficult to build a line through it.

The tramway appeared to be built from a hodgepodge of materials and could only support a narrow-gauge engine and log cars. When these narrow-gauge cars connected with the B. B. & B. C., they had to be reloaded on the necessary 'right-sized' cars.

One can see by the attached map that the Mogul-Tramway Spur had quite a quantity of miles of track since each section is one-mile square. Little information is available concerning this spur system.

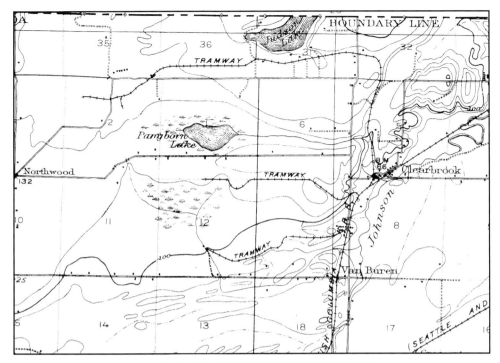

MOGUL-TRAMWAY SPUR LAYOUT

The Mogul-Tramway apparently had a large portion of Whatcom County all to itself. There are no records available that indicate the ownership of this area, and it was assumed that the system was used exclusively for the logging of mainly cedar trees. (E. Erickson)

MOGUL-TRAMWAY TRACK

The track as shown is certainly different than any other railroad track in the area. It was thought by some to be a streetcar track. This roadbed, complete with the track, can still be located in a few places in the defined area. (R. Perry)

MOGUL-TRAMWAY LOG TRAIN

This logging train is said to be a mismatch of materials, from narrow-gauge rail to a variety of other types of equipment. (M. Impero)

Chapter 5
Engines and Other Equipment

Due to the demand for railroad equipment and construction items throughout the whole country, the development of the Bellingham Bay and British Columbia Railroad got off to an extremely slow start. Being stuck in this remote area of the corner of Washington State made the situation even worse. In the construction of the railroad, B. B. & B. C. was forced, in many cases, to buy used rail, often lighter than what the design called for, that caused future problems.

JJ Donovan recognized the problem immediately when he took over the reins of the railroad. The need for all the construction items and rollingstock was obvious.

First to arrive in Sehome were Engines #1 and #2, along with assorted other equipment. It became evident that the railroad shop facilities needed to be enlarged so they would have the ability to make a variety of railroad cars and other equipment. Very rapidly the question surfaced: Were the roadbed and structures previously constructed adequate for the increased size of equipment that was planned to be purchased?

Within weeks upon arrival in Sehome in 1899, JJ reported to Cornwall in San Francisco a list of rollingstock that would be needed soon. His list included: (20) log-trucks, (40) 25-ton airbrake gondolas, (10) 25-ton air brake flats, and (1) Mogul Locomotive, with 60,000-pound drivers. Donovan got the go ahead from San Francisco and ordered 10 flat cars immediately.

Dated February 27, 1903, this was an article published in the *Whatcom Reveille* newspaper:

The new Baldwin Consolidated Freight Locomotive recently purchased by the B. B. & B. C. arrived in Fairhaven over the Great Northern on Wednesday afternoon. This locomotive was described in a recent issue of the Reveille. Before being put into service, a few changes will be made at the B. B. & B. C. roundhouse. The driving wheels will be turned, coal burning grates will be put in place, and a spark arrestor and air pump will be installed. The locomotive will be ready for the run in about two weeks.

Another *Whatcom Reveille* article dated April 10, 1903:

The new locomotive #8, recently purchased by the B. B. & B. C. Railroad, will go on the freight run between Whatcom and Maple Falls today. This is the heaviest locomotive that has ever come to the bay. It is a consolidation engine manufactured by the Baldwin Locomotive Works of Philadelphia, PA. The cylinders are 20 inches in diameter and have a 24-inch stroke. The boiler pressure is 130 pounds. The weight of the engine alone is 133,000 pounds and the weight of the engine and tender, ready for service, is 213,000 pounds.

Considerable work has been done on the engine in the local shops of the Company. It has been converted from wood to coal burner by changing the grates and placing in a spark arrestor on the front end. An air pump has been put on for train brakes and the water capacity of the tender increased from 28,000 to 38,000 gallons of water.

The work on the extension of the B. B. & B. C. is moving rapidly and the trains will be running six miles above Maple Falls within a short time. The passing track at Strandel Station has been torn up and will be replaced with heavier rails.

In ordering the above-named equipment, JJ soon realized that they would need to enlarge their shop facilities and start making these major pieces of equipment in-house in Sehome. JJ did what he always did, he pushed the throttle full speed to get the facility in high gear.

Bellingham Herald article dated November 25, 1903:

GREAT IMPROVEMENT TO THE RAILBED IN ORDER TO CARE FOR THE HEAVY TRAFFIC AND NEW EQUIPMENT, ALL MODERN AND THAT IS OF THE HIGHEST QUALITY

One of the busiest short lines in America is in this county with its terminal in Bellingham. This road is the Bellingham Bay and British Columbia. Everyone cognizant of the facts will admit the truth of the assertion.

The facts used in this article were obtained from Master Mechanic W. J.

McLain of the B. B. & B. C. today. Mr. McLain says it is certainly true that this railroad has a business equal to any road of its length and territory of any in the United States.

W. J. McLain has held the position of Master Mechanic of the B. B. & B. C. for the past six years, and he states that the improved conditions of equipment by the line, as well as freight and passenger cars, this year is certainly wonderful.

BIG GROWTH SHOWN

Six years ago, Mr. McLain says that only four men were employed in the car shops, engaged in taking care of the shops and doing repair work, while now there are fifty. The monthly payroll at that time was $300 and is now $2800. The locomotive engineers' payroll was $270 a month, is now $1200.

Next year the company contemplates building several observation cars and more freight cars. The observation cars will be used in carrying excursions to the end of the line in the Mount Baker District. The business of the road is so extensive now that Mr. McLain says there is hardly enough cars commensurate with the traffic, which will necessitate additional cars. These cars will be built in the B. B. & B. C. car shops during the winter. An important adjustment to the operation is the mechanic shops.

ROADBED IS IMPROVED

The roadbed on the mainline between Whatcom and Sumas has been substantially improved for heavy traffic. Nearly all the trestles have been filled in and heavy rails have been laid on account of the heavy rollingstock now in use on the road.

BIG MACHINE SHOP

Important adjuncts to the railroad operation are the B. B. & B. C. machine shops. Machinery is now being made in this department for the Nooksack Falls Power Plant and being installed by the Bellingham Bay Improvement Company. The shops contain a 65-inch lathe, one of the largest in the Northwest. It is a new Rac Edgers, the patent of which is owned by the B. B. I. C. and is being manufactured in the shops.

Beginning next year, it is quite probable that the steamers owned by the Alaska Packers' Association will be brought to this point to have the machinery repaired at these shops. The shops are equipped with pneumatic borers, a hydraulic press, and a large power hammer. Four fires are kept burning steadily in the blacksmith shop. Five years ago only but one fire was necessary.

OWNS VAST CAR PLANT

A visit to the B. B. & B. C. car shops is an interesting scene. A force of carpenters under the foremanship of E. E. Sherwood is at work on the construction of new boxcars for the road to be used in carrying shingles from the mills to the various states in the Union. The shops turn out an average of three cars a week that weigh 31,000 pounds and have a carrying capacity of 60,000 pounds. The inside dimensions are length, $36^1/_2$ feet; width, $8^1/_2$ feet; and height, $8^1/_2$ feet. Every car is equipped with regulation air brakes and automatic couplers.

In the month of September 1904, W. J. McLain reported additional information:

A total of 176 cars is required to operate the business of the road. Equipment now consists of eight locomotives, one being purchased this year, a Baldwin of the heavy freight type, weighing 170,000 pounds, 9 passenger coaches, 93 flat cars, 6 small boxcars and 14 large ones, 16 pairs of logging trucks, and one large steam shovel. The company now has an order of 50 new boxcars to be filled at the B. B. & B. C. car shop.

The machine shops have also been rushed with work. Engine #1 has been equipped with steam brakes, Engine #7 given a general overall, Engine #6 rebuilt, with a new engine tender built, and Coaches #3 and #7 painted and revarnished.

The new logging caboose is nearly complete and will soon be placed in use. Coach #3, which is being rebuilt for a mail and baggage car, is finished with the exception of painting and will be placed on the line next week.

The B. B. & B. C. Railroad is about to unveil their new mail car. A new baggage and mail car will soon leave the shops in Bellingham. It is an old combination mail, baggage, and smoking car practically rebuilt and is in as good shape as new. It will attract attention as soon as it is placed in service owing to its color. It is being painted and the color scheme is pink with gold lettering on the outside. The car will make its debut in about ten days. As soon as it is appearing on the track it will be the cynosure of all eyes, for there is no car on the railroad lines west of the Mississippi that will be as pretty as our #3.

Also added to the line is a Fairbanks Morris Motor Car #1 which will be used as an inspection car. It is a two-seater, four-wheeled, single engine car. A locomotive engineer used to take the road master on inspection trips to check the tracks and so forth. Now that can all be done from the motorcar.

Another unique passenger coach has been added to the line. This coach is a M–2 McKeen Motor Car manufactured by McKeen Motor Car Company. This 70-foot motor car is powered with a 250 hp gas engine. Within a few months after receiving the car the company will place it in service between Bellingham, Lynden, and Sumas. The McKeen car will not be able to provide service to Glacier because of the steeper grades on this route.

The B. B. & B. C. Railroad car shop in Bellingham built the first cars to be used on the extension. These modern cars, ten in number, were constructed with standard air brakes and automatic couplers. Six old flat cars were rebuilt in lengths from 34 feet to 36 feet with the entire body of each car overhauled. The new flat cars weighed 23,500 pounds with a carrying capacity of 60,000 pounds. The top of the cars set on pressed steel trucks.

Master Mechanic W. J. McLain provided additional information:

A funeral car at a cost of $5000 and a water car for the Whatcom County Railroad and Light Company were constructed. The Railroad Gazette of Chicago requested Mr. McLain to give a special description of electric motors built in their shop as well as photographs, which will appear in the current issue of the Gazette.

A roster of equipment that was held by the Bellingham Bay and British

Columbia Railroad at this time listed a total of nine locomotives, with #1 being built by the H. J. Booth & Co., and the remaining #2 through #9 constructed by the Baldwin Locomotive Company.

The amount of equipment that was owned by the B. B. & B. C. Railroad varied greatly from time to time. The only equipment that was actually owned were their locomotives, construction equipment, and a range of railroad cars. Many cars that were being moved on to the B. B. & B. C. could have been from different railroads all over the country. The prime example of the railroad moving local cars that were owned by other entities within Whatcom County were the ore cars which belonged to Olympic Portland Cement Company. These were hauled from the Limestone Station to the cement plant on Marine Drive.

The following is a list of equipment that appeared in *Bulletin No. 84* in 1906:

Passenger equipment:
(1) Mail and Baggage Car (1890), (1) Combine (1891), (1) Combine (1892), (2) Coaches (1891), (2) Coaches (1902)

Freight Equipment
(56) Box Cars (6 acquired 1889, 50 built 1903-04), (102) Flat Cars, (1) Tank Car, (24) Logging Trucks, (12) Other Cars (maintenance, etc.), (3) Cabooses, (9) Locomotives

When the Chicago, Milwaukee, St. Paul, and Pacific took over the ownership of the B. B. & B. C., the locomotives and all the other equipment would change drastically.

BELLINGHAM BAY AND BRITISH COLUMBIA - ENGINE #1
Engine #1, nicknamed "D. O. Mills," was built in 1868 by the Union Iron
Works for hauling coal. At that time, it was known as #3 on the Black
Diamond Railroad. H. J. Booth & Co. was the builder and the production
number was #9. The specifications were: Type 0-6-0, Cyls. 14" x 18",
Drivers 36". The #1 burned wood, using a sunflower stack. It began operation
in Bellingham on October 11, 1884, and was first used on construction, then on
freight and log trains. Her first engineer was Harry Abbott, an Englishman.
(D. Jones)

BELLINGHAM BAY AND BRITISH COLUMBIA - ENGINE #2
The B. B. & B. C. Engine #2 had the nickname "Black Diamond" and was
built in 1870. It was also bought used from the same source as #1. Upon
arriving in Whatcom, Master Mechanic Taggart performed a major rebuild of
the engine. The "Black Diamond" was built by the Baldwin Company, Serial
#2141, Type 0-6-0, Cyls. 15" x 22", Drivers 44". In 1906 she was sold or leased
to the McCush Columbia Valley Logging Company of Kendall. The front
nameplate marked "Rebuilt B. B. & B. C. 1892," was found at the site of the
Silver Lake Manufacturing Company north of Maple Falls. (D. Jones)

BELLINGHAM BAY AND BRITISH COLUMBIA - ENGINE #3
Engine #3 was purchased brand new from the Baldwin Works in 1891 by
the B. B. & B. C. Railroad: Serial #11517, Type 4-4-0, Cyls. 17" x 24",
Drivers 62". She was well-known in the Northwest, beginning with a long
career of passenger service. In the early 1900s, she was converted to coal with
the tapered stack and later to oil burning. It had symmetrical headlights that
were later changed to cylindrical ones. The #3 was wrecked on a logging grade
on the Kulshan Branch on her last trip under the care of her first engineer,
Jack Treutle. He was making his first trip down the heavy grades on this
branch with an 18-inch pump and was unable to hold his train. JJ Donovan
wrote a memorial to Jack found in the later chapter identified as "Accidents
and Disasters." (D. Jones)

BELLINGHAM BAY AND BRITISH COLUMBIA - ENGINE #4

Engine #4 also was bought brand new from the Baldwin Company in 1891. A smart, fast engine, it was a fine example of the extended wagon top, the firebox, and low boiler stack Baldwin moguls of the period. The engine was Serial #12,231, Type 2-6-0, Cyls. 17" x 24", Drivers 54". This engine was used on way-freight and passenger runs. She dropped her crown sheet in Sumas under B. & N. operation, killing the fireman. (D. Jones)

BELLINGHAM BAY AND BRITISH COLUMBIA - ENGINE #5
Engine #5, built in 1881 for the Union Pacific Railroad by Hicks Locomotive and Car Works, was sold to B. B. & B. C. in January 1900. First used on the run with log trains and then for years on the Lynden local, it was "owned" by Engineer William Shorey. Engine #5 was another Baldwin engine: Serial #5943, Type 2-8-0, Cyls. 19" x 24", Drivers 50". (D. Jones)

BELLINGHAM BAY AND BRITISH COLUMBIA - ENGINE #6
Engine #6 was a Baldwin Vauclain Compound 2-8-0 bought from Hicks Locomotive and Car Works. This Baldwin was extremely heavy with a total weight of approximately 125,000 pounds, Serial #13,800, Type 2-8-0, Cyls. 13$\frac{1}{2}$" & 23" x 24", Drivers 50". Built in 1893 it was used on way-freight and long trains. She dropped her crown sheet on Cougar Hill in the fall of 1905. It was transferred to Tacoma by Chicago, Milwaukee, and St. Paul after 1926. (D. Jones)

BELLINGHAM BAY AND BRITISH COLUMBIA - ENGINE #7
This engine was bought from Hicks Locomotive & Car Works by the
Bellingham Bay and Eastern Railroad in 1902 to be used on line construction
from Silver Beach to Wickersham. On completion, she was bought by the
B. B. & B. C. and gave long service as a switcher and pusher in Bellingham,
with occasional trips on passenger, freight, and long trains. It was a Baldwin
Type 4-6-0, Cyls. 18" x 24". (D. Jones)

BELLINGHAM BAY AND BRITISH COLUMBIA - ENGINE #8
Engine #8 was purchased from Hicks, having been built as the "Koo-Ley-Cui-Tan" for the Simpson Logging Company on Hood Canal, where she pushed and pulled logs between the rails. A powerful engine, she was converted to coal with a straight stack. For three years she was the Road's principle freight engine, pulling the daily log trains, and then sold in 1926 to Heinz Lumber Company, Seneca, Oregon. The engine was a Baldwin Type 2-8-0, Cyls. 20" x 24", with 54" Drivers. (D. Jones)

BELLINGHAM BAY AND BRITISH COLUMBIA - ENGINE #9
Engine #9 again was a Baldwin, built in 1908 for mixed service, and was the third engine bought 'new' by the road. This Baldwin was Type 4-6-0 and transferred to Tacoma by C. M. & P. S. (D. Jones)

ENGINE #4
Engine #4 in the rock cut of the Goshen/Kulshan Branch. (D. Jones)

**CHICAGO, MILWAUKEE, ST. PAUL, AND PACIFIC RAILROAD
DIESEL LOCOMOTIVE**

After the Chicago, Milwaukee, St. Paul, and Pacific Railroad purchased the Bellingham Bay and British Columbia Railroad, in a short period of time all of the steam locomotives were replaced with diesel. Many of those old and antiquated steam engines were sold to customers such as logging camps, but the bulk of all of them were sold to scrap yards. (T. Schnepf)

STANDARD BELLINGHAM BAY AND BRITISH COLUMBIA BOXCAR
Boxcars came in a variety of lengths. The length of this particular car is not known. The total number of the boxcars that were owned by the railroad was fifty-six in 1906. Many were made at their own yard, and others were purchased from manufacturers. (Whatcom County Museum)

Specifications of North Coast Box Car
(CAPACITY 40 TONS)

Gauge, 4 feet, 8½ inches.   Length over End Sills, 40 feet, 10 inches.   Width over Side Sills, 9 feet, 1½ inches.   Width inside. 8 feet, 6 inches.   Height inside, 8 feet, 0 inches.   Width of Door Opening, 6 feet. 0 inches.   Height from Rail to center of Coupler, 2 feet, 10½ inches.   Height from Rail to Top of Floor, 4 feet, 1 inch.

Red Fir used throughout for woodwork of the car.

Six Sills 5 x 9 inches.

Four Truss Rods, 1½ inches round.

Automatic Couplers and Tandem Spring Draft Gear.

Westinghouse Automatic Air Brake.

Standard Two-Ply Roof with prepared Roofing Paper between the two courses.

Security Door Hangers.

One End Door

Cast Steel Body Bolsters.

Malleable Iron Post and Brace Pockets.

Trucks, Rigid Diamond Frame Arch Bar Type.

Cast Steel Bolsters.

Steel Channel Spring Plank.

Wheels, 33-inch Chilled Cast Iron.

Steel Axles with 5 x 9 Journals.

Malleable Iron Journal Boxes.

Inside Hung Metal Brake Beams.

NORTH COAST BOX CAR
(Seattle Car and Foundry Company, Catalog #503, Page 40)

Standard Low-Logging Flat Car

(80,000 POUNDS CAPACITY)

Equipped with Hercules Patent Bunk and Knight Patent Chock

Gauge, 4 feet, 8½ inches.   Length over End Sills, 41 or 42 feet.   Width over Side Sills, 8 feet, 6 inches.   Height from Rail to Top of Deck, 3 feet, 6 inches.   Height from Rail to Top of Bunk, 4 feet.   Height from Rail to Center of Coupler, 2 feet, 10½ inches.

This car is specially designed for heavy service, with extra heavy Red Fir Sills and Decking, and strongly trussed.

End Sills are protected by Steel Plate on face.

Steel Body Bolsters specially designed for Low Logging Car.

Automatic Couplers with Side Unlocking Lever and Standard Draft Gear, with either Tandem or Twin Springs.

Automatic Quick-Action Air Brake, with hand Brake arranged to work either vertically or horizontally.

As shown in illustration, this car is equipped with Hercules Patent Bunk and Knight Patent Chock, and consequently stake pockets are not necessary, but when required, malleable iron pockets with closed backs are furnished.

LOW-LOGGING FLAT CAR
(Seattle Car and Foundry Company, Catalog #503, Page 32)

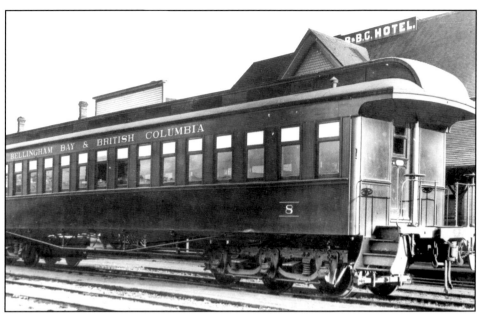

BELLINGHAM BAY AND BRITISH COLUMBIA PASSENGER CAR

The B. B. & B. C. fleet of passenger cars totaled four in 1906. Some of the cars were built in the Bellingham shop and others were purchased. Also, some were 90% steel while others, particularly the passenger parts, were all from wood. Passenger cars #4 and #5 both had seating capacities of 52, while #8 had a capacity of 66. The combination passenger, baggage, and mail coach #5 had a capacity of 32. (D. Jones)

**BELLINGHAM BAY AND BRITISH COLUMBIA CABOOSE
AND PASSENGER CAR**

The picture shows a typical combination of a caboose and a passenger car. A portion of the caboose was used for baggage. At one time the railroad had three cabooses. (D. Jones)

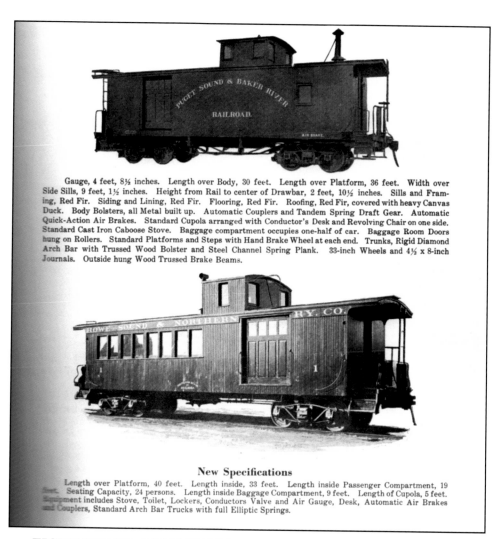

Gauge, 4 feet, 8½ inches. Length over Body, 30 feet. Length over Platform, 36 feet. Width over Side Sills, 9 feet, 1½ inches. Height from Rail to center of Drawbar, 2 feet, 10½ inches. Sills and Framing, Red Fir. Siding and Lining, Red Fir. Flooring, Red Fir. Roofing, Red Fir, covered with heavy Canvas Duck. Body Bolsters, all Metal built up. Automatic Couplers and Tandem Spring Draft Gear. Automatic Quick-Action Air Brakes. Standard Cupola arranged with Conductor's Desk and Revolving Chair on one side. Standard Cast Iron Caboose Stove. Baggage compartment occupies one-half of car. Baggage Room Doors hung on Rollers. Standard Platforms and Steps with Hand Brake Wheel at each end. Trunks, Rigid Diamond Arch Bar with Trussed Wood Bolster and Steel Channel Spring Plank. 33-inch Wheels and 4½ x 8-inch Journals. Outside hung Wood Trussed Brake Beams.

New Specifications

Length over Platform, 40 feet. Length inside, 33 feet. Length inside Passenger Compartment, 19 feet. Seating Capacity, 24 persons. Length inside Baggage Compartment, 9 feet. Length of Cupola, 5 feet. Equipment includes Stove, Toilet, Lockers, Conductors Valve and Air Gauge, Desk, Automatic Air Brakes and Couplers, Standard Arch Bar Trucks with full Elliptic Springs.

EIGHT WHEEL COMBINATION BAGGAGE CAR AND CABOOSE
(Seattle Car and Foundry Company, Catalog #503, Page 51)

LOG HAULING TRUCKS

Long log hauling trucks were used to haul logs of various lengths. The spacing of the trucks could be down to 10 and 12 feet or up to 100 feet. Upon being dumped at the mill site or a mill pond, two trucks could be connected for the return trip to the woods. Logs, of course, were also hauled on flat cars.
(D. Jones)

**Equipped with Knight Patent Chock
Block and Cast Steel Bolster**

CODE
"Herksteel"
Number 127

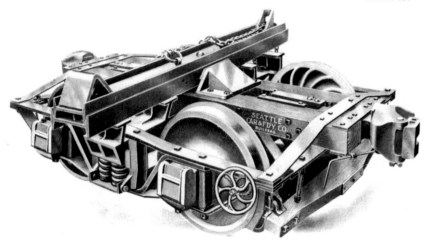

Hercules Logging Truck

A STEEL TRUCK OF 80,000 CAPACITY THAT HAS CARRIED 120,000 SAFELY

This is a steel frame truck, with cast steel bolster and bunk brace, and is here shown with structural bunk, but may be equipped with cast steel bunk of either the Hercules, McLafferty or Skookum patent, and also with steel draft beams, making an all steel truck.

Heavy Bar Shear

33-inch Chilled Cast Iron Wheels and Steel Axles, with 4½x8 inch Journals. Height from rail to center of Drawbar, 25½ inches, and to top of Bunk, 40½ inches. Length over Draft Beams, 9 feet, 6 inches.

Automatic Couplers with Bottom Unlocking Attachments. Brake Shoes applied to all Wheels, with hand wheel at side or hand lever at end. Weight, approximately 18,000 pounds per set.

HERCULES LOGGING TRUCK
(Seattle Car and Foundry Company, Catalog #503, Page 14)

BELLINGHAM BAY AND BRITISH COLUMBIA LOGGING TRAIN CAR AT KENDALL

This type was identified as a skeleton logging car and was used the most for normal length logs. (E. Erickson)

BELLINGHAM BAY AND BRITISH COLUMBIA McKEEN MOTOR CAR

B. B. & B. C. owned and operated one McKeen Motor Car as a passenger and mail vehicle between Bellingham, Lynden, and Sumas. It could not operate to Glacier because some of the grades were too excessive. (D. Jones)

McKEEN MOTOR CAR COMPANY

The McKeen Motor Car Company of Omaha, Nebraska, was a builder
of internal combustion engine railroad motorcars, constructing 150 cars
between 1905 -1907. Two lengths, 55 and 70 feet, were offered and could
accommodate 64 or 205 passengers respectively at a top speed of 55 mph.
The cars were equipped with between 100 and 300 hp gasoline motors. They
were not equipped with reverse gearings; so, to reverse the car, the motor ran
backwards. McKeen were generally wood paneled on the interior and fitted
with transverse bench seats with a center aisle. The rounded rear was fitted
with a semicircular bench seat. Lighting was originally acetylene.
(Internet photo)

No. 15-B Fairbanks-Morse Inspection Motor Car

WEIGHT, 1200 LBS. PACKED FOR EXPORT, 2000 LBS.

No. 15 Motor Car with canopy top. The canopy top is not included in the regular equipment, but can be supplied at an extra price when desired.

SPECIFICATIONS

Wheels.	22-inch diameter, wood center.
Axles.	1½-inch steel, which are placed inside 2¼-inch tubing with roller bearings.
Brake.	Trussed brake wooden shoe operated by foot lever.
Seating Capacity.	Four people. Leather upholstering; frame, steel and wood carried on springs.
Power	Single cylinder vertical engine, about 6 horse-power.
Transmission.	Planetary type, liberally constructed. Gears running in oil, giving two forward speeds and one reverse.
Ignition.	By jump spark.
Lubrication.	A system of forced feed lubrication is used. It is entirely automatic and needs no attention other than that of filling the tank once a week when car is in use.
Speed.	The maximum speed of the car is about thirty miles per hour. The speed, however, is under perfect control from this down to three or four miles per hour.
Gasoline.	Uses ordinary stove gasoline; car carries enough to run 100 miles.
Code Word.	With canopy top, Motrop.

B. B. & B. C. INSPECTION MOTOR CAR
(E. Erickson)

BELLINGHAM BAY AND BRITISH COLUMBIA STEAM SHOVEL
The railroad records indicated that the B. B. & B. C. had only one steam
shovel, although one would have thought that they would have had more. The
early railroad grades were constructed by men and horses pulling scrapers.
(D. Jones)

STEAM POWERED PILEDRIVER
This photo shows an example of a piledriver. In this case, it is mounted on a sled and pulled along. Pilings were cut out of quality trees and were stood up and driven into the ground to support a structure. (E. Erickson)

Chapter 6

Depots and Other Buildings

The Bellingham Bay and British Columbia Railroad had a multitude of different depots and buildings throughout the line. From the warehouse buildings down on Sehome Dock to the station in Glacier, there was a great variety of structures and uses.

The Sehome Dock was owned and operated by the railroad, and in the early days, the bulk of all incoming and outgoing freight came through this seaport.

All the buildings needed for the construction and repair of engines and cars were in one general area right at the south end of what is now Railroad Avenue. At this point there were machine shops, foundries, engine repair shops, and any other operation vital to the well-being of the railroad. Also, at this location was a roundhouse that was used for many years. Along the line there could have been a series of buildings that were designated for light repair and storage, but the bulk of all the maintenance and repair went on in Bellingham.

The buildings along the line came in a variety of styles and construction quality. A masterpiece of appearance and operation, the Bellingham Station was an example. Small stations or depots along the line, in some cases quite crude with no windows or doors, were used for passenger convenience and a small amount of storage.

Another showplace was at the end of the line in Glacier. This high-quality Glacier building had all the accommodations of a full station building. It appears that the station manager and his wife took particularly good care of it, including large beautiful flowerpots all around the structure. Unfortunately, the building burned down prematurely in the "Great Fire of Glacier" in 1915. However, it was completely rebuilt at the same place, at the same size, and in the same style, including the same flowerpots.

The small depot buildings along the line were of great use in the beginning because of the high demand for passenger traffic. As time went on, with more people owning automobiles, using improved roads, and not traveling by train, needed maintenance of these structures did not happen. In a matter of a few years many of these depots were completely removed.

The buildings along the line that continued to be part of the operation were reasonably maintained and updated. Many of these were also used as post offices and telegraph offices.

In addition, the Bellingham Bay and British Columbia Railroad did enter Canada and had a depot at Huntington, situated just across the border from Sumas.

B. B. & B. C. Railway Station, Bellingham, Wash.

BELLINGHAM BAY AND BRITISH COLUMBIA RAILROAD STATION
BELLINGHAM, WASHINGTON

Bellingham Station was a large, three story building. The first floor had a sizable waiting room and a baggage and express room. It also housed the dispatcher, operator's office, train register, bulletin board, a place for picking up train orders, and a marker board. There was a large boiler room adjacent to the baggage room where the coach cleaners and janitors stored equipment. The second floor contained offices for the superintendent, roadmaster, auditor and clerks, traffic department, and civil engineering departments. Filing and storage was on the third floor. The above photo was hand-colored and the true color is not known. (D. Jones)

**WASHINGTON DOUGLAS FIR LOG IN FRONT OF BELLINGHAM
B. B. & B. C. STATION**
Compare this hand-colored photo to the one on the previous page. (D. Jones)

COMPLETE WESTSIDE VIEW OF BELLINGHAM STATION
The B. B. & B. C. Hotel is on the left with the station to the right. Sehome
Mountain is to the right of the station. One can date the photo by the horses in
the lower right. (D. Jones)

SOUTHWEST VIEW OF BELLLINGHAM BAY AND BRITISH COLUMBIA STATION

The hotel, barely visible to the north of the station, was used as a hub for people traveling through the area. They could come in by ship or by other trains and then travel out to different destinations. (T. Schnepf)

NORTH END OF B. B. AND B. C. RAILROAD STATION

This view shows the covered walkway around the building. The B. B. & B. C. Railroad constructed a hotel adjacent to the station, and a corner is shown on the left side of the picture. The hotel proved not to be highly successful and was demolished in 1924. (T. Schnepf)

B. B. & B. C. STATION FREIGHT OFFICE
Both men behind the desk appear to be involved in the paperwork of the freight office. One would assume that the one to the extreme left is the freight manager. (D. Jones)

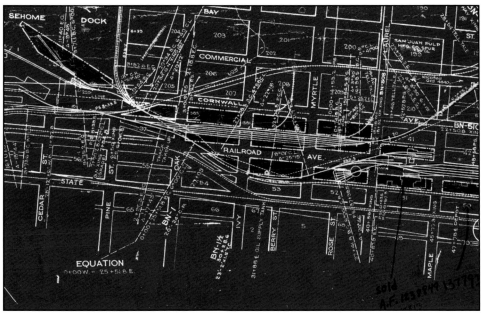

THE TWO B. B. & B. C. LINES MERGED NEAR SEHOME DOCK
The dark boxes just below Cornwall Avenue were on the Squalicum Creek, or Lower, Route. Those below Railroad Avenue were on the original High Route. All the dark boxes represent railroad owned working properties.

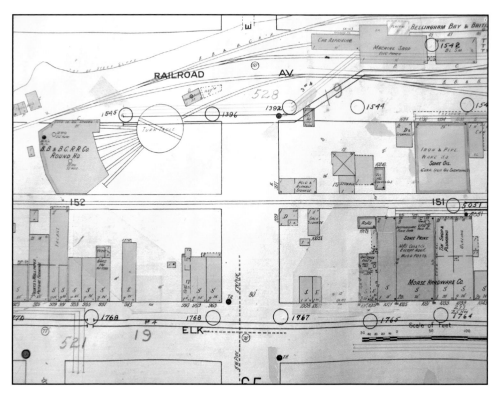

ORIGINAL FACILITIES OF B. B. & B. C. RAILROAD IN BELLINGHAM
This map shows the end of Railroad Avenue down in the area of today's
Depot Market and Bellingham's Farmers Market. Near the top of the photo is
Railroad Avenue and at the bottom of the picture is Elk Street [State Street].
The structure in the left of the picture is the roundhouse and storage building
for the engines. Above that, where the word railroad appears, are the tracks
that would lead down to the Sehome Wharf. (Center for Pacific Northwest
Studies – W.W.U.)

Milwaukee Road Roundhouse
Bellingham, Washington 1974

BELLINGHAM BAY AND BRITISH COLUMBIA ROUNDHOUSE
The location of the roundhouse is shown in the previous page. Once the engine was parked on its "bridge," it could be rotated 180 degees. This roundhouse was turned by a crew pushing it around. (D. Robson)

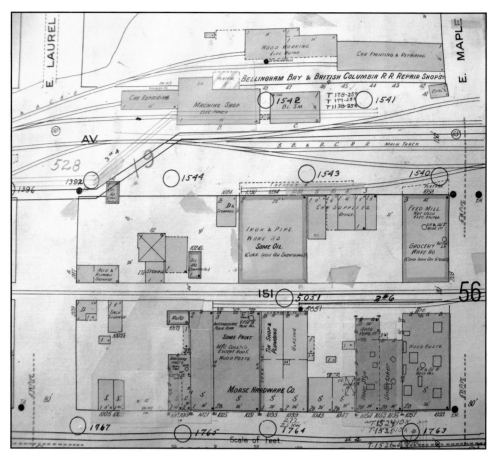

LAYOUT OF B. B. & B. C. RAILROAD MAINTENANCE BUILDINGS
Railroad maintenance buildings are at the top of the page above the railroad tracks. At the bottom of the photo are the facilities of the Morse Hardware Company. (Center for Pacific Northwest Studies – W.W.U.)

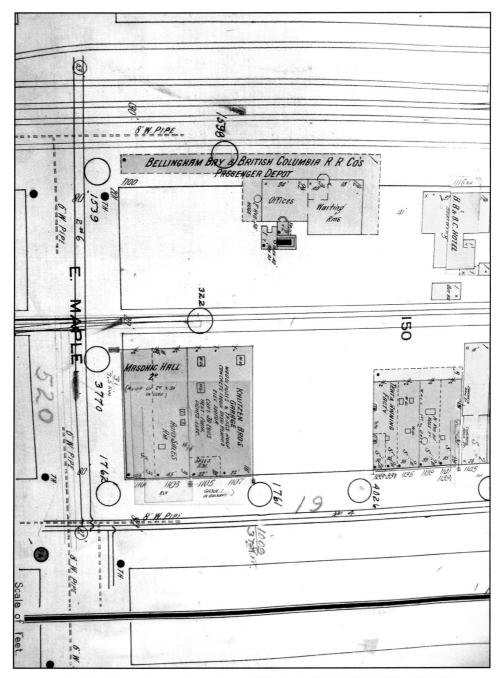

LOCATION OF B. B. & B. C. RAILROAD STATION AND HOTEL
The Bellingham Bay and British Columbia Railroad Station and Hotel were situated at the intersection of Railroad and Maple Streets. Today the site is occupied by the Depot Market. (Center for Pacific Studies – W.W.U.)

Stations and Distances from Bellingham

PLACE	Distance Bellingham.	How Connected	Car Capacity
SUMMIT	A 2	E and W..	20
SCUDDER	3	1 E...	6
SQUALICUM	4	1 W...	4
DEWEY	5	1 W...	4
HONEY	A 5	1 W...	6
VAN WYCK	5.8	W.6E.	15
NOON, NO. 1	7	1 W.	12
NOON, NO. 2	A 7	1 E...	4
BADGER	8	E and W...	10
WAHL	8.9	1 W...	8
CARROLL	10	1 W...	14
GOSHEN	10.6	E and W..	20
CENTRAL	12.7	1 W.	8
RENOLDS	13	1 W...	6
McDONALD	A 13	1 W...	5
MILLERTON	14	1 W...	12
STRANDELL SIDING	15.1	E and W...	22
NORDSTROM	A 15	1 E...	10
STRANDELL SPUR	B 15	1 E...	9
EVERSON	15.8	1 E...	7
HAMPTON	17.1	E and W..	20
VAN BUREN	19	1 W...	2
H'NTON	A 19	1 W...	4
MOGUL	20	1 W...	4 mi.
CLEARBROOK	A 20	E and W.	20
HAVERSTICK		1 W...	
SUMAS	23.3	Yard...	50
HAWKINS	24	1 E.	7
BOLCOM	A 24	1 E.	6
LAMPERTON	25.5	E and W..	10
ALLEN NO. 2.	26	1 E.	4
PALMER	27	1 W...	4
SAAR CREEK	A 27	1 W...	3
PETERSON	A 29	1 W...	2
COLUMBIA	30.8	E and W..	20
DEVON	33	1 W...	10
KENDALL	A 34	E and W...	20
BAXTER	35	1 W...	4
WATSON NO. 1	35	1 W...	6
WATSON NO. 2	36	1 W...	6
HAMILTON	A 36	1 W...	2
WAYLAND	B 36	1 W...	2
BIGELOW	C 36	1 W...	3
MAPLE FALLS	37.2	Yard...	20
ASPLUND	38	1 E...	6
SIMMONS	40.	1 W...	5
MILLER	40	1 W...	6
WARNICK	41.9	1 W...	3
THURSTON	A 42	1 E..	5
NESTOS	43	1 W...	6
CORNELL	44	1 W...	3
GLACIER	44.2	Yard...	8

LYNDEN LINE.

PLACE	Distance Bellingham.	How Connected	Car Capacity
SWIM	L 20	1 E...	5
WORTHEN	M 20.8	E and W..	10
GRAVEL PIT	N 21	1 E...	12
ROO	O 22	1 W...	9
MORRISON	P 22	1 W...	3
LYNDEN	Q 22.7	Yard.. ...	25

*No Agent.

STATIONS AND DISTANCES FROM BELLINGHAM
This chart is believed to show all the stations/depots beyond Bellingham and on the Lynden Line. There would have been spurs off spurs, but these are believed to be the main lines. (W. Gannaway)

TELEPHONE HOUSE AT SQUALICUM JUNCTION
One thing that the Chicago, Milwaukee, and St. Paul Railroad did upon purchasing the B. B. & B. C. Line was to send out a professional photographer to provide a complete visual recording of what was included in the sale. At that time, it would be assumed that all communications throughout the line were through a telephone system. This would have replaced the telegraph.
(T. Schnepf)

DEWEY DEPOT

Proceeding north, the Dewey Depot was located approximately five miles up the line from Bellingham. Some of the stations had available a waiting room, an agent operator room, and a warehouse. No attempt has been made to illustrate all the depots or stations on the line. The ones that were selected had some significant record. (T. Schnepf)

VAN WYCK DEPOT

The Van Wyck Depot was located at the point where the B. B. & B. C. crossed the Van Wyck County Road. It was not named after an original homesteader pioneer in the area, but after one of the early superintendents for the railroad. (T. Schnepf)

NOON DEPOT

The Noon Depot was located where the Noon Road and the railroad crossed down in Noon Valley. At this location, there were spurs both on the west side and east side of the track; one serving a shingle mill and the other a sawmill. In this valley Gus Bellman homesteaded 160 acres and created Bellman Gardens. These gardens became very prosperous and provided goods for much of the population in the Bellingham area and points south. When the B. B. & B. C. approached Bellman about a right of way through his property, he was eager for this mode of transportation and charged one dollar for the right. The railroad provided a means of getting his vegetables into Bellingham and hauling horse manure from the Kentucky Street Stables out to the farm. (T. Schnepf)

GOSHEN DEPOT
Goshen had a full-time agent who lived in the adjacent railroad house. Note the metal milk cans setting out front between the tracks. Also note that the building had chimney pipes and was much more sealed up. The left end was used for a post office. (T. Schnepf)

SECTION MAN'S HOUSE - GOSHEN
Note the piled railroad ties and fire-killed snags to the left. (T. Schnepf)

CENTRAL DEPOT
Most depots were constructed where the railroad crossed county roads.
Central was located where it intersected Central Road. (T. Schnepf)

EVERSON DEPOT
The Everson Depot was the first real full-service depot north of Bellingham.
Note the ticket window in the center, the Wells Fargo Express Freight sign,
and the metal milk cans. In the early days of service, the passenger business
was a major part of their income. (T. Schnepf)

HAMPTON DEPOT

Hampton was the location on the line where the Lynden Branch headed west
to Lynden. One can see that this depot is somewhat more modern and has a
closed end. It was built later than the others on the way to Sumas. (T. Schnepf)

LYNDEN DEPOT AND END OF LYNDEN BRANCH

The Lynden Depot was constructed later than the other major depots and
was also more modern. It had a large waiting room, a freight room, and an
agent operating room. In addition, there was a feature that all depots north of
Bellingham did not have, an inside toilet facility with a tub. Later, the depot
was moved two blocks east toward Hampton. (D. Jones)

Largest Creamery in the State Lynden, Wash.

LYNDEN CREAMERY

The picture identifies this creamery to be the largest in the state of Washington, and it seems quite fitting that it would have been located in Lynden. Note all the wagonloads of milk cans which appear to be waiting to be unloaded. The single can shown is a totally different situation. (W. Gannaway)

CLEARBROOK DEPOT

Clearbrook was the next station and at one time had an agent. This site had a passing track for feeding trains and unloading cars, etc. The Mogul Line extended several miles into the north country near the Canadian border and many loads of logs, shingles, and other wood products were harvested in this area. Clearbrook and Kendall were both small communities that were created by the arrival of the B. B. & B. C. Railroad and experienced similar rapid growth with hotels, stores, and schools. However, both died as ghost towns within 20 years. (Sumas Library)

SUMAS DEPOT

Sumas Depot had passenger waiting room, inside toilet, freight room, and an office for the agent and his helpers. At one time it included a large steeple. There was also a small stall roundhouse or engine shed. Mister Gilman was the material clerk and was stationed in a building near the 'Y'. In the lower left corner of the picture you can see the U.S./Canadian Line. This line crosses the tracks almost horizontally and represents the actual location of the border. (D. Jones)

SUMAS DETENTION HOUSE

This structure was located near the International Border in Sumas. It was identified as a detention house and was included with the Chicago, Milwaukee, and St. Paul index of pictures. One possible use could have been as a holding center for illegal immigrants crossing the border. The following is a paragraph from the *Coroner's Register #1, Whatcom County, Washington*, compiled by Linda K. Larson. *P. 180 June See (a woman's name) - April 26, 1908, - no jury - found at Gov. detention house at Sumas. Age 21. Buried by John Gillies of Sumas Remarks: Deceased came to her death by having her throat cut by Lee Wing Wah.* (T. Schnepf)

INSPECTION OF CHINESE AND BAGGAGE AT SUMAS DEPOT
(Sumas Library)

HUNTINGTON DEPOT
The Bellingham Bay and British Columbia and the Chicago, Milwaukee, and
St. Paul had agreements to cross into Canada. The extent of these agreements
is not known, but as seen in the above picture, probably freight and passengers
were delivered going in both directions. (T. Schnepf)

TYPICAL RAILROAD WATER TANK

Water was one of the most important commodities to be used in the early days of steam trains, such as the time when the B. B. & B. C. was created. Without a source of water, the train would come to a complete stop. These tanks were spaced along the railroad and all steam trains typically stopped for a refill. The job of keeping these tanks functioning was a major responsibility of the section crew. This tank was located in Everson. (T. Schnepf)

LIMESTONE JUNCTION DEPOT

This depot was located within the 'Y' that took traffic into the limestone quarry from the mainline going up the valley. Rock shipments were actually the last products shipped down out of the Columbia Valley area. (T. Schnepf)

KENDALL DEPOT

The Kendall Depot appears to be quite complete, although it did not have a full-time agent. One can look at the right side of the picture and see that the structure has had an addition. (T. Schnepf)

KENDALL DOUBLE OUTHOUSE
With doors, it would be assumed that this outhouse was for the use of the
workers and the passengers. Maybe not. (T. Schnepf)

KENDALL SECTION MEN'S HOUSE
This typical section crew house was located in Kendall. Each section of the
railroad had an assigned crew, and the ones near Bellingham obviously lived
in Bellingham. However, in situations like Kendall, housing was provided.
A section crew was made up of a foreman and three men who maintained a
certain portion of the rail line. (T. Schnepf)

ASSORTMENT OF BUILDINGS AT MAPLE FALLS DEPOT, 1903
At the Maple Falls Depot of the B. B. & B. C. Railroad looking east in 1903,
one would see the depot, tracks, boxcars, various sheds, and the water tower.
(Whatcom County Museum)

MAPLE FALLS DEPOT, 1903
When the railroad reached Maple Falls the town already existed, so it was
not created like Kendall. Unlike most small towns up the North Fork of the
Nooksack, Maple Falls was rough and tumble, made up of loggers, miners,
and apparently a group of men that seemed to have been rejected from other
spots, contributing to its share of murders. The depot is currently a residence
in Maple Falls. (Whatcom County Museum)

GLACIER STATION
Glacier was the end of the Bellingham to Glacier Run. (T. Schnepf)

EAST VIEW OF THE GLACIER STATION
This view of the station shows the three-story Mountain Home Hotel to the
right. People traveling through the area stayed in the hotel, but it was mainly
used by railroad employees. (T. Schnepf)

GLACIER STATION AGENT HOUSE
The station agent obviously had an energetic wife judging by all the details
shown here. (T. Schnepf)

REAR VIEW OF TRAINMEN'S GLACIER HOUSE
This is another example of housing provided in Glacier for railroad workmen.
Some of these structures had a very crude look within a short period of time.
One can tell this structure did not have a woman's input. (T. Schnepf)

GLACIER SECTION MEN'S HOUSES
It is obvious that the further up the line one went, conditions became worse for
the workers. (T. Schnepf)

GLACIER ENGINE HOUSE
The engine house was the building in which the engine was stored overnight or for longer periods of time. The building was heated by wood and the fire in the boiler of the engine was kept burning. (T. Schnepf)

CHICAGO, MILWAUKEE, AND ST. PAUL DEMING DEPOT
This is a photo of the Deming Depot on the Goshen-Kulshan Branch. Ernie Henderson is the agent in the center. Later, the depot was moved to Kulshan where it was situated within the 'Y' turnaround. It acted as a depot and a general storage area, as well as the post office from December 12, 1916, to February 15, 1918. Canedy Herbert was the postmaster. (D. Jones)

ABANDONED BELINGHAM STATION

At a point in time the Bellingham Station was abandoned, along with many of the other buildings that were created at the end of Railroad Avenue. A new passenger and freight station was relocated down Railroad Avenue at the site of the current La Fiamma – Wood Fire Pizza restaurant. (Whatcom County Museum)

**DEMOLITION OF THE BELLINGHAM BAY AND BRITISH COLUMBIA
BELLINGHAM STATION**

The Bellingham Station was built in 1892 by the Bellingham Bay and British
Columbia Railroad and was demolished by the Chicago, Milwaukee, and
St. Paul Railroad in 1942. The station serviced the area and people for over
50 years. (Whatcom County Museum)

Chapter 7

Train Operation

PASSENGER TRAIN OPERATION

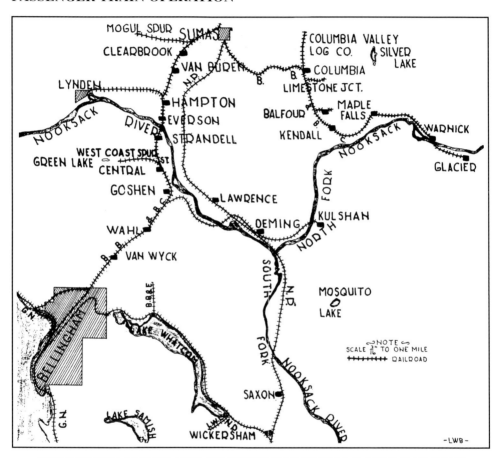

BELLINGHAM BAY AND BRITISH COLUMBIA RAILROAD MAP
This simplified map shows the routes of the B. B. & B. C. Railroad. The second train line from the left running north/south is the Northern Pacific (N. P.). (*BULLETIN No. 84, Railroad & Locomotive Historical Society, Inc. - W. Gannaway*)

BELLINGHAM BAY AND BRITISH COLUMBIA RAILROAD COMPANY

TRAINS WEST					Distance from Glacier	Capacity of Sidings	Schedule No. 34 — Taking Effect June 1, 1907, One O'Clock A.M. — STATIONS	Distance from Bellingham	TRAINS EAST					Water, Coal, Scales, Table and Wyes
PASSENGER No. 10 FIRST CLASS SUNDAY ONLY	PASSENGER No. 8 FIRST CLASS SUNDAY ONLY	MIXED No. 6 SECOND CLASS DAILY EXCEPT SUNDAY	MIXED No. 4 SECOND CLASS DAILY EXCEPT SUNDAY	PASSENGER No. 2 FIRST CLASS DAILY					PASSENGER No. 1 FIRST CLASS DAILY	PASSENGER No. 3 FIRST CLASS DAILY EXCEPT SUNDAY	MIXED No. 5 SECOND CLASS DAILY EXCEPT SUNDAY	PASSENGER No. 7 FIRST CLASS SUNDAY ONLY	PASSENGER No. 9 FIRST CLASS SUNDAY ONLY	
Ar. 6.45 p.m.	Ar. 8.00 A.M.	Ar. 4.55 P.M.	Ar. 9.45 A.M.	Ar. 11.10 A.M.	44.2	200	BELLINGHAM	.0	De. 4.10 P.M.	De. 5.20 P.M.	De. 10.15 A.M.	De. 7.10 P.M.	De. 8.30 a.m.	T and W...
•6.38	7.53	•4.40	•9.30	•11 02	41.5	20	SUMMIT 3-7	2.7	•4.17	•5.28	•10.30	•7.17	•8.37	
6.30	F 7.47	F 4.25	F 9.15	F 10.55	38.4	15	VAN WYCK 3-1	5.8	F 4.25	F 5.35	10.55	F 7.25	F 8.45	
6.22	7.40	4.05	8.55	10.46	35.3	8	WAHL 1-7	8.9	4.34	5.45	11.20	7.34	8.52	
6.17	7.35	3.55	8.45	10.41	33.6	20	GOSHEN 3-1	10.6	4.39	5.50	11.30	7.39	8.56	
F 6.12	F 7.30	F 3.45	F 8.33	F 10.36	31.5	4	CENTRAL	12.7	F 4.43	F 5.55	11.40	F 7.43	F 9.00	
F 6.07	F 7.25	3.35	8.23	F 10.30	29.1	22	STRANDELL 3-4	15.1	4.49	F 6.05	11.50	F 7.48	F 9.05	
6.03	7.20	3.30	8.08	10.25	28.4	7	EVERSON 0-7	15.8	4.53	6.10	12.10	7.52	9.10	
6.00	7.15	3.25	7.55	10.20	27.1	20	HAMPTON 1-3	17.1	4.56	6.15	12.20	7.55	9.14	
	7.40		F 7.40		30.2		WORTHEN 3-1	20.2		F 6.30				
			De 7 30 A.M.		32.4	25	LYNDEN	22.4		Ar. 6.45 P.M.				Y
5.52	7.07	3.15		F 10.12	24.2	20	CLEARBROOK 2-8	20.0	F 5.05		12 40	8.02	9.22	W
De. 5.45 P.M.	7.00	De. 3.00 P.M.	De. 10.03 / Ar. 9 35	9.20	20.9	50	SUMAS 3-3	23.3	Ar. 5.15 / De. 5.45		Ar. 1.00 P.M.	De. 8.10 / 8.20	Ar. 9.30 a.m.	Y, S and C
	F 6.48		F 9.20		18.7	10	LAMBERTON 3-3	25.5	F 5.55			8 27		
	F 6.42		F 9.10		16.4		NICOLAY 3-0	27.5	F 6.07			8.35		
	6.33		9.00		13.4		COLUMBIA 3-3	30.8	6.20			8.43		
	6.27		8.50		10.2	20	KENDALL 3-3	34.0	6.35			8.52		
	6.20		De. 8.35 / Ar. 8.05		7.0	20	MAPLE FALLS 3-4	37.2	Ar. 6.55 / De. 7.20			9.02		W and Y
	F 6.13		F 7.55		4.6		KULSHAN 3-3	39.6	F 7.33			9.07		
	F 6.06		F 7.45		2.4	3	WARNICK 3-4	41.8	F 7.40			9.15		
	De. 6.00 a.m.		De. 7.35 A.M.		0		GLACIER	44.2	Ar. 7.50 P.M.			Ar. 9.20 p.m.		T

(Vertical note: No. 1 will not run east of Sumas on Sundays / No. 2 will not run east of Sumas on Sundays)

West Bound Trains are Superior to East Bound Trains of the Same Class.

SPECIAL RULES.

F—Flag Station. •—Trains do not stop for Passengers. Full-faced Figures (1, 2, 3) denote meeting and passing points.

Register Stations—Bellingham, Hampton, Lynden, Sumas, Maple Falls and Glacier.

Yard limits at Bellingham extend from North switch. at Summit, to all track South.

Sumas yard extends from Boundary Line to 1000 feet South of South leg of Wye, and to N. P. crossing on North Fork Extension. All except First Class Trains will not exceed speed of eight miles per hour in yard limits.

Abbreviations:—W—Water; S—Scales; C—Coal; Y—Wye; T—Table.

SPECIAL RULES.

Note Change in Rules. Standard Rules Govern and Must Be Understood by All Concerned.

Trains will not exceed schedule time between Columbia and bridge No. 4, and must be kept under control approaching curves where slides are liable to occur.

Air brake cars must be coupled next locomotive. Hand-brakes must be applied on all cars not provided with air-brakes before descending the grade between Columbia and Lamberton.

Speed over truss bridges and high trestles must not exceed 15 miles per hour.

All Trains and Engines must come to a full stop at all R. R. crossings at a distance not exceeding 200 feet from same.

BELLINGHAM BAY AND BRITISH COLUMBIA SCHEDULE, JUNE 1, 1907

On this map, a depot between Maple Falls and Glacier was identified as Kulshan. However, this is not the same Kulshan as identified on the Goshen to Kulshan Branch. (W. Gannaway)

A *Bellingham Herald* newspaper article dated December 19, 1905, concerning Uncle Jerry read:

This morning Uncle Jerry Daniels is being sheltered from the rain and the wind by a little house erected on Railroad Avenue for this purpose. Hereafter, when he is not occupied with waving his red flag as a warning to pedestrians, he can occupy his little house and be sheltered from the elements. The Council last evening granted a petition to the Bellingham Bay and British Columbia Railroad officials, and the house was erected promptly this morning. It is a small affair, but large enough for protection, has a little flagpole, and is nicely painted in brown and red.

BELLINGHAM BAY AND BRITISH COLUMBIA RAILROAD

MAIN LINE—BETWEEN BELLINGHAM AND GLACIER

MT. BAKER
THE PARADISE
OF
AMERICA

Reached via
GLACIER,
and the New Scenic
MT. BAKER TRAIL

VAST SNOW FIELD!
MAMMOTH GLACIER!
DEEP CREVASSES
GORGES, RAPIDS,
WATERFALLS

HEALTHFUL
AND INVIGORATING
ATMOSPHERE

An Ideal Place
for a Summer Outing

WEEK END
EXCURSION FARES

FARMING
DAIRYING
FRUIT GROWING
POULTRY RAISING

UNLIMITED
OPPORTUNITIES
IN THE
FERTILE
NOOKSACK VALLEY

EXTENSIVE
IN AREA

RICH IN SOIL
AND
CLIMATE

For Particulars, Address
Traffic Department

READ DOWN / **READ UP**

STATIONS (Main Line):
BELLINGHAM, Dewes, Van Wyck, Noon, Wahl, Goshen, Central, Standell, EVERSON, Hampton, Van Buren, Clearbrook, SUMAS Lv., SUMAS Ar., Lumberton, Nicolay, Columbia, Balfour, MARIETTA FALLS, Limnos, Warnick, GLACIER

BETWEEN BELLINGHAM AND LYNDEN

STATIONS:
BELLINGHAM, Worthen, LYNDEN

BETWEEN SUMAS AND LYNDEN

STATIONS:
SUMAS, Hampton, Worthen, LYNDEN

f Flag Station—trains stop on signal.
* Account of limited baggage space, company reserves the right to forward baggage on later trains when necessary. The time from midnight to noon is shown in light-faced figures, and from noon to midnight in heavy-faced figures.

BELLINGHAM BAY AND BRITISH COLUMBIA RAILROAD SCHEDULE

This is an example of a B. B. & B. C. Railroad schedule. The schedules were constantly changing, and the date of this one is not known. In the beginning the bulk of train usage was passengers; and then as time went on, it became more of a freight situation. In this schedule one can see that the Goshen to Kulshan line did not exist. (T. Warger)

163

PASSENGERS WAITING AT CLEARBROOK STATION
Passengers were waiting for a special train. The locomotive shown was
B. B. & B. C. #3. The photograph was taken by the well-known Bellingham
photographer by the name of Sanderson. (Whatcom County Museum)

ELEGANTLY DRESSED PASSENGERS BOARDING THE TRAIN
The railroad ran special excursion trains for special events; however, this
occasion is not identified. (Whatcom County Museum)

BELLINGHAM BAY AND BRITISH COLUMBIA PASSENGER COACH
This is a passenger train in route to Glacier. If you look at the front coach near
the right end, you will see it is Coach #8. (Whatcom County Museum)

PASSENGER TRAIN PASSING IN FRONT OF VAN WYCK DAIRY
The train is traveling down Dewey Valley between Wahl Depot and Noon
Depot. (I. Park)

HIGH BRIDGE OF SAAR CREEK CANYON
Locomotive #5 is stopped on the highest of the bridges in the canyon, and the passengers are out enjoying the view. (Whatcom County Museum)

Bellingham Bay & British Columbia
RAILROAD.

Pass

1899

Until December 31, 1899, unless otherwise ordered.

No. 1

GEN'L SUPERINTENDENT.

BELLINGHAM BAY AND BRITISH COLUMBIA RAILROAD PASS
This pass was designated for the year 1899, and if you look in the lower left corner you can see it is Pass #1. (Whatcom County Museum)

BRIDGES OF SAAR CREEK CANYON
The four bridges in the canyon frequently allowed scenic stops for passenger trains. (Whatcom County Museum)

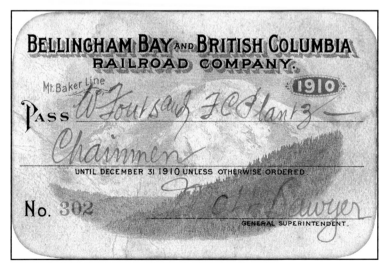

BELLINGHAM BAY AND BRITISH COLUMBIA PASS, 1910
This 1910 pass was issued to W. Fouts and F. C. Plantz, Chairmen. It would be accepted on both passenger and freight trains. (Whatcom County Museum)

FIRST EXCURSION TRAIN

WHATCOM TO HARDAN

Saturday, May 18, 1901

WILL RUN AS FOLLOWS:

SOUTH					NORTH			Miles from Whatcom
Arrive 6:10 P. M.,			WHATCOM	Leave	9:00	A. M.		
"	5:35	"	GOSHEN	"	9:33	"		11.
"	5:20	"	EVERSON	"	9:45	"		15.9
"	5:00	"	SUMAS	"	10:10	"		23.3
"	4:40	"	LAMBERTON	"	10:20	"		25.5
"	3:30	"	HILLTOP	"	11:30	"		29.7
"	3:15	"	KENDALL	"	11:45	"		34.2
Leave 3:00		"	HARDAN	Arrive 12:01	P. M.			37.5

Engine will give three long whistles five minutes before leaving Hardan and also five minutes before leaving Saar Creek Canyon between Lamberton and Hilltop, where a stop of about one-half hour will be made both going up and coming down.

Passengers desiring to visit the Fish Hatchery one mile south of Kendall, will leave the train at that station at 11:45 A. M., and be ready to take the return train at 3:15 P. M.

J. J. DONOVAN,
Gen. Supt.

EDSON & IRISH, PRINTERS, WHATCOM.

FIRST EXCURSION TRAIN
The first excursion train went from Whatcom to Hardan (Maple Falls) on Saturday, May 18, 1901. Two items in this are worth mentioning: first, the B. B. & B. C. was only complete to Hardan, and the name had not been changed to Maple Falls; second, it also stated that an opportunity to visit the fish hatchery near Kendall was planned. (Whatcom County Museum)

SPECIAL EXCURSION, 1906
This is an advertisement for a special excursion from Bellingham to Lynden on July 4, 1906. (Whatcom County Museum)

Bellingham Herald Article June 23, 1908:

The residences of Kendall, Maple Falls, and Glacier are entitled to a better train service than the Bellingham Bay & British Columbia Road is now giving them. The management is giving them a train four days a week because the business does not warrant a better *service. For a big corporation this seems like a small policy. The line from Sumas to Glacier has contributed thousands of dollars to the company in the past and will be a great money maker in the future. It happens that the slump in the lumber business makes the traffic along the line very light at the present time, but not so light that*

**BELLINGHAM BAY AND BRITISH COLUMBIA RAILROAD
MT. BAKER BROCHURE**
The railroad worked diligently with others such as the Chamber of Commerce to promote the Mount Baker National Forest. (*Maple Falls Leader*)

the company is justified in refusing to give the hundreds of people in the three towns a daily mail and passenger service. Just now there is a prospect of a revival of the lumber business; activity will begin in the cement plant; rush of the miners to the Mount Baker District has begun; hundreds of campers are preparing to go to the hills; and a big church camp meeting will be held in Maple Falls this summer. Their movements demand a better service. If the road is going to follow the policy of running daily trains every once in awhile when it has enough traffic to make it pay, its popularity will not increase rapidly.

During 1912 and 1913 a passenger train ran out of Glacier leaving at 7:30 a.m. daily except Sunday and returned to Glacier daily at 6:45 p.m. All these trains had a mail car or baggage car, and carried such items as milk, express freight, ice cream, crates of eggs, and boxes of fruit. Besides the engine and train crew, the train had a mail clerk, a baggage man, and a newsboy. The Saturday night train leaving Glacier would pick up passengers at different stations, including workmen from logging camps and shingle and sawmills who were going home. Other passengers aboard were musicians going from one town to another for dances.

An article from the *Maple Falls Leader* newspaper dated December 28, 1926, shared the following information: *The train the other day made the amazing time of 37 miles in five hours, or 7²/₅ miles per hour, between Bellingham and Maple Falls. It will be remembered that Stevenson, who invented steam engines, railroads, etc., could travel 5 miles an hour with ease. He could speed up to 15 miles an hour, but ordinances, etc., were in force prohibiting joyriding above 5 mph. There are no speed ordinances along this line, so there is no limit to speed. A train is at liberty to best Stevenson's record of 15 mph, if it feels sporty.*

FREIGHT TRAIN OPERATION

BELLINGHAM BAY AND BRITISH COLUMBIA FREIGHT CARS
This is a scene of Railroad Avenue in downtown Bellingham where many railroad cars were stored between the perpendicular streets. Straight ahead would have been the station and Sehome Dock. (Whatcom County Museum)

LOGGING TRAIN WITH MASCOT
This is B. B. & B. C. Locomotive #2. It had been leased out to the McCush
Logging Company of Columbia and Kendall. (*The Fraser Valley Challenge*, p. 87)

BELLINGHAM BAY AND BRITISH COLUMBIA FLATBED LOG CAR
This is a typical log train moving on a spur track heading for the mainline.
(Whatcom County Museum)

WHATCOM COUNTY TOOTHPICK

The old-growth forests of Douglas fir and western red cedar in Whatcom County were famous for their enormous trees. Forty-nine different railroad logging companies operated during this period. (D. Jones)

ANOTHER WHATCOM TOOTHPICK

One of the problems in transporting the log as shown is the difficulty in making relatively sharp turns because of the long length. They had to be quite selective which railroad spur was traveled. (Black Mountain Forest Center)

SHAY LOGGING LOCOMOTIVE

The Shay locomotive was almost exclusively owned by timber companies and used for logging operations. The Shay was capable of going up and down steep grades safely, and operated at a slower speed, thus not being used on mainlines. (Black Mountain Forest Center)

YARDER BEING TRANSPORTED BY RAIL

A logging yarder "donkey" is being transported by rail. The weight of some of these machines is unbelievable. All the early yarders were powered by steam; this one is powered by a diesel engine. (Black Mountain Forest Center)

GLACIER LOG RELOAD
In the middle of World War II there was a shortage of fuel for road logging trucks. The trucks were allowed to transport the logs out of the forest and down to Glacier. At this point they were offloaded and then reloaded on railroad cars to complete the trip. There were two reload operations in Glacier. (D. Hamilton)

LOADING RED CEDAR SHINGLES IN BOX CAR

Timber products that were commonly shipped by the Bellingham Bay and British Columbia Railroad were logs, sawn lumber, and cedar shingles. The cedar shingles were cut from old-growth red cedar, packed, and bundled as shown in this picture. They were one of the most used roofing products on the West Coast. (Black Mountain Forest Center)

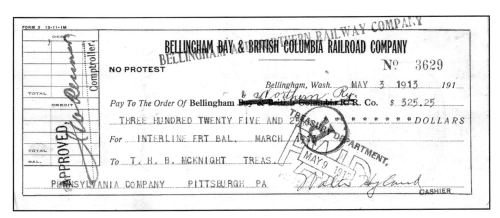

PAY VOUCHER TO BELLINGHAM BAY AND BRITISH COLUMBIA RAILROAD

This check for $325.25 is from Pennsylvania Company in Pittsburgh, Pennsylvania. (W. Gannaway)

BELLINGHAM BAY AND BRITISH COLUMBIA FREIGHT INVOICE
This commodity invoice is for fishnet and rope freight from New Whatcom to
Blaine. The 'Back Charge' listed as $85.93 could be from a previous bill that
had not been paid. (W. Gannaway)

BELLINGHAM BAY AND BRITISH COLUMBIA RECEIPT #4051
This is just one of many forms that were used by the B. B. & B. C. Railroad
in its daily operation. The date on this document is September 25, 1901.
(Whatcom County Museum)

The above barge carried twelve cars loaded with general yard stock from the Larson Lumber Co. plant at Bellingham, Wash.

CHICAGO, MILWAUKEE, AND ST. PAUL RAILROAD BARGE SYSTEM
When the Chicago, Milwaukee, and St. Paul Railroad purchased the Bellingham Bay and British Columbia Railroad in Whatcom County, they had no rail rights with other railroads. To transport freight south, it had to be shipped by water. This barge system was called the Milwaukee Terminal Railroad Company. Down at the Sehome Dock Milwaukee constructed a ferry slip and loaded and unloaded railcars using a locomotive. (D. Jones)

TYPICAL LOGGING RAILROAD CREW
The man on the left was Roscoe Murrow, the father of Edward R. Murrow
who gained national fame as a World War II news commentator. (D. Jones)

Most freight carloads consisted of lumber products: shingles, shingle bolts, lumber, logs, piling, and cordwood. Other types of freight were grain, hay, flour, potatoes, milk, etc.

Campbell River Logging Company of Canada shipped 50 to 60 carloads of logs per day. These logs were inspected and bonded by the customs in Sumas and shipped to Bellingham, unloaded at the log dump, and towed by tugboat in log booms back to mills in Canada.

The most important employee on a railroad train was the conductor. He was totally responsible for putting a train together with a combination of freight and passengers. Almost everyone in its operation and movement answered to him.

The average daily wages for railroad employees on the Pacific Coast Commercial Railroads were listed as follows:

Station Agents	$ 2.20
Enginemen	$ 4.58
Firemen	$ 2.55
Conductors	$ 3.77
Section Foremen	$ 1.92
Trackmen	$ 1.42
Telegraph Operators & Dispatchers	$ 2.53
Laborers	$ 1.99
Office Clerks	$ 2.40

Chapter 8
Accidents and Disasters

TYPICAL TRAIN DERAILMENT
A derailment in the days of the B. B. & B. C. Railroad, particularly on a spur line, was a quite common occurrence. It would appear to be a monumental task to get the engine back on the track, but it occurred so often that the rail crew was very efficient. (R. Perry)

A man by the name of Hyman had a terrible fall and narrowly escaped losing his life while working on the high bridge in Saar Creek Canyon on the branch of the B. B. & B. C. to Glacier. The bridge was 70 feet tall and Hyman fell from the top staging area down to the third deck, from there he would have fallen to the rocks below had not one of his fellow workmen caught hold of him as he struck the deck. He was badly bruised about the head, had dislocated ribs, and his elbow was broken. The injured man was removed

to Sumas where the local doctor did all in his power to relieve the suffering. He then was brought to the Bellingham hospital.

In 1905 a train wreck was narrowly averted on the Bellingham Bay and British Columbia Line near Warnick. With the wheels of the front truck blocked, a large log train was standing on the tracks near the Glacier Station awaiting the arrival of the engine. However, while the last car was being loaded, the blocking was in some manner dislodged; and the heavily loaded train started on the downhill grade for Maple Falls, gathering speed until it was going fully 30 miles an hour. Some of the train's crew who were aboard the logging cars were powerless to stop it. The wild ride continued some five or six miles until the upgrade was reached in the Maple Falls area and the train stopped five minutes before the scheduled time for the passenger train #1 to reach that point. Only for the fact that the passenger train was delayed at Maple Falls was a serious accident avoided.

The B. B. & B. C. Railroad train was derailed, blocking the route from noon until 10:30 one night above Sumas. A derailment of two log trucks occurred at milepost 27 in Saar Creek Canyon.

Caused by the extremely long length of the train, a flange on a wheel of one of the trucks broke as the train moved slowly around the curve. Just as the first of the four rear trucks went off the track, the engineer and the crew of the caboose discovered the accident. They uncoupled the caboose and put on the brakes so that it was saved and no one was hurt. The accident happened five miles above Sumas and it took the work crew from early in the morning until 10:30 at night to clear the way. One set of the trucks was replaced on the track without unloading the logs, but the others were not so easily handled. The afternoon train from Glacier, due to return to Bellingham at 4:00 p.m., did not get through the accident site until late at night. It was 5:30 the next morning before it returned to the city.

James Moore met with an accident at Glacier when a can of gasoline ignited and exploded. Moore, engineer of the Bellingham Bay and British Columbia Railroad Engine #3, was seriously burned by the explosion and brought to Bellingham on a special train, arriving at 11 o'clock that night. Fortunately, his wounds were not considered to be life threatening. The next day it was reported that he was resting easy; and it was believed that, unless for complications, there was little doubt of a speedy recovery. According to the statements of those who were with him at the time the accident occurred, Moore had entered the roundhouse after his regular trip to Glacier and discovered the can of gas, which he carried on the train. He attempted to place its capping cork more firmly in place, apparently without thinking of the impending danger. The gasoline was suddenly ignited, and an explosion followed. Although his clothing was set on fire, quick movement on his part extinguished the flames without him sustaining great injury. Moore had been in the employment of the railroad company for about eight years and was considered one of the most careful and trustworthy engineers on the road. He and his family lived at 211 Unity Street.

Mr. Berguson, 40 years of age, switchman in the employment of the Bellingham Bay and British Columbia Railroad Company, was almost instantly killed about 10 o'clock one morning on Railroad Avenue near Laurel Street in the neighborhood of the Bellingham Bay and British Columbia Roundhouse. Just how the accident took place was not learned since there were no eyewitnesses. Berguson was an experienced railroad man and had been in business with the B. B. & B. C. Company for upwards to five years. Coming to the city from Omaha, he was believed to have been engaged in the usual performance of his duties at the time when he was struck by a car and completely mangled. Medical assistance was called at once, and within a minute or so the ambulance had been summoned and Dr. Kirkpatrick was on the scene. Everything possible was done for the stricken man, but he expired ten minutes later just as he was being lifted aboard the ambulance. He was a married man with one child. A formal investigation into the circumstances surrounding the accident began that afternoon, and all the members of the yard crew were called to give evidence.

An accident occurred on March 13, 1913, in Sumas when Engine #4 exploded. Russel Golithan, the fireman on the Bellingham and Northern, was badly scalded and immediately taken to Clark Hospital in Sumas. He died that morning at about 6 o'clock without regaining consciousness. Engine #4 had been overseeing the Bellingham and Northern Work Train and was running on a sidetrack at Sumas, detached from the remaining cars and caboose, with the fireman left in charge of the locomotive. At 12:30 in the morning the sound of a terrible explosion was heard. The members of the crew, who were sleeping in the caboose, rushed out and saw the locomotive enveloped in flames. Golithan was unconscious and so badly scalded that it was evident from the first that he could not survive.

In 1913 a man identified as Gibson was fatally injured by a train. A former deputy sheriff, he was working as a brakeman on Bellingham and Northern when hit by a car at Hinton's spur, about 20 miles from Bellingham, while coupling two cars. After coupling had been made, Gibson gave the signal for the engineer to slack the train. He fell and was struck by one of the cars. That afternoon he was brought to Bellingham and placed in St. Joseph Hospital, treated by Dr. Key and Dr. Shute.

MOUNT BAKER 1911 MARATHON RACE TRAIN DERAILMENT
During the 1911 Mount Baker Marathon, Engine #3 struck a bull and, along with the combination baggage car/Coach #4, was derailed and overturned. (G. Byeman)

TRAIN DERAILMENT BY HITTING A LARGE BULL ON TRACK
Harvey Haggard, standing second from the left in what appears to be a robe, was a contestant in the first marathon race; and up until the train wreck, he was the leader. There were two routes for the marathon. On one route the contestants were delivered to Glacier and then went by foot up the Mount Baker Trail to the summit. The other was up the Middle Fork Trail to a starting point at the Heister Ranch and then on foot to the summit. The rules of the race stated that you could use any form of transportation to get to the start of the trail. Participants that used the Mount Baker Trail chose a train ride, and a special one was provided. For the other route, transportation was provided by automobiles to the start of the trail. (G. Byeman)

GRAND CELEBRATION FOLLOWING THE RACE
BARBECUING THE BULL

Haggard continued his return to Bellingham from the train wreck, first in a horse and buggy with one of the wheels falling off. Then he borrowed a horse and rode the rest of the way to the finish line. For all his effort, he came in second place. "Betsy," the car that the winner rode in, is shown to the left. (G. Byeman)

LOCOMOTIVE DERAILMENT BULL

A giant bull derailed the train returning from Glacier with Haggard, one of the marathon runners, aboard. Haggard was leading the race and would have won if not for the bull. It was decided to have a large picnic the following day, and the bull, quite tender by this time, was barbecued and served. (D. Jones)

On May 11, 1916, one of the most respected train engineers in Whatcom County, John C. Treutle, was killed on the McCoy-Loggie Logging Road when brakes on Locomotive #3 failed to operate. Treutle, of Bellingham, was killed instantly that Saturday morning at about 8 o'clock when he lost control of his train east of Welcome and collided with two cars loaded with logs. A veteran engineer and widely known, he was hauling gravel cars down a grade when the accident occurred.

After the train had gathered speed, it was found that the brakes would not operate. Everyone jumped except him. He was getting ready to jump from the locomotive when it struck the log cars and tipped over, the cab going to one side of the track with the boiler to the other. He was an old employee of the Bellingham Bay and British Columbia Railroad, and a strange coincidence of the accident was that he was the first engineer to drive the locomotive which caused his death. Engine #3 was owned

"THE GREAT TRAIN WRECK" - BELLINGHAM AND NORTHERN RAILROAD

"The Great Train Wreck of 1916" occurred near Cornwall Park on August 23 when two trains of the Bellingham and Northern Railroad collided. Bert Plough, engineer on the work train, was injured, but the rest of the train crew jumped before the impact and were unhurt. Freight #63 was the heavier of the two trains and managed to push the work train about 200 feet after the impact. (D. Jones)

WRECK OF BELLINGHAM AND NORTHERN ENGINE #3
This wreck killed engineer Jack Treutle who was a very long-term engineer and most respected by all in the railroad community. The accident occurred on May 11, 1916, on the Kulshan Branch near Welcome. The train was coming down a logging grade and he lost air for his brakes. (D. Jones)

by the Bellingham and Northern and leased to the logging company a few days earlier. He was survived by his widow and three daughters. Treutle had come to Bellingham nearly 30 years earlier, previously being an engineer in West Virginia.

JJ Donovan, Vice President of the Bloedel Donovan Lumber Company and former Superintendent of the railroad, wrote the following tribute to Jack Treutle and Engine #3:

A PIONEER IS GONE

Jack Treutle is dead! Today all Masonic Brothers pay their last tribute to a simple, honest man. He died as he lived - on duty. It was a strange incident that he should go to his end on the locomotive which he drove first when it came new and bright from Baldwin shops nearly 30 years ago – B. B. & B. C. No. 3. He has held the throttle on many of engines since then, and few men were better known in the Northwest country. For many a day he will be held in loving remembrance in mining and logging camps and our own railroad caboose. He stays with his engine till the last and none suffered but himself. God rest his soul! JJ Donovan

On May 16, 1937, the worst disaster in the history of the Bellingham Bay and British Columbia and the Chicago, Milwaukee, St. Paul, and Pacific

Railroads occurred. The scene of this tragedy took place approximately $1/8$ of a mile east of Maple Falls on the mainline. The accident occurred on a 70 to 80-foot-high bridge spanning Maple Creek Canyon.

The railroad crew had moved a piledriving derrick mounted to a flat car out near the center of the bridge and was preparing to work over the side. In preparation to start the work, half of the crew was down on the canyon floor and the remainder up on the bridge proper. As the machine had been swung around over the side, the operator started to lower the hammer and follower in the piledriving leads, and the brake apparently slipped. With the hammer freefalling, the operator dogged the brake causing the sudden stop to throw an excessive weight over the side. With that the derrick tumbled off the bridge. The main reason for the accident was thought to be that the operator failed to follow the required rule of attaching the derrick to the flatcar and then to the opposite side of the trestle.

Four workers from the railroad company were killed: Leslie Titus, 47, Falls City, Fredrick Worstman, 58, Sumas, Otto Johnson, 38, Seattle, and William Burrell, Spokane. William Deckert, 53, Bellingham, survived with a broken back. At the second that the machine started to tumble over the edge, one member of the crew heard a cracking sound and shouted a warning. This warning probably saved four other men from their deaths. Titus was trapped under the boiler of the machine and was scalded to death.

Several train cars of men rushed from Deming to the scene of the accident to render assistance. Raymond Karwaski, the only local man working on the piledriver, happened to be the signal man for the day, so he escaped injury. Terrified men rushed from Maple Falls trying to extract the men from beneath the broken derrick. A bulldozer from Skyline Timber Company was also rushed to the scene, clearing away the debris and making the removal of the bodies possible. Collins, a fireman, had just stepped from the derrick to the coal and water tender, the cars uncoupling as they fell. Lonnie Smith, another worker, gave a warning cry in time to save some of the men working below the derrick. Hearing his cry, they were able to run to safety.

Robert Heller was a student at Maple Falls Grade School, located about a half mile from the accident scene. At that point he knew nothing about what had happened, but heard a bulldozer running down the county road at a high speed. The bulldozer operator was hoping to assist in any way that he could.

After all these years, down in the canyon floor, there remain sections of sheet metal from the accident.

Following the closure of the railroad beyond Maple Falls, the Duronso Brothers Shake Mill of Kendall salvaged the piling and lumber from the trestle.

MAPLE FALLS RAILROAD TRAGEDY
This view is from the bridge deck looking straight down into the canyon where one can see the twisted destroyed equipment. (D. Haddock)

FIRST EVERSON BRIDGE WASHED AWAY

The first B. B. & B. C. Railroad bridge crossing the Nooksack River at Everson was of an extremely poor design. This pile bent bridge could not resist the turbulent water of a winter runoff and was washed away in 1900. It was replaced with a two-span wood truss bridge that lasted until it was burned down. (Whatcom County Museum)

WELCOME BRIDGE COLLAPSES INTO NOOKSACK RIVER
This bridge was built as a covered railroad bridge by the Chicago, Milwaukee, and St. Paul Railroad for the St. Paul and Tacoma Lumber Company. In 1944 it was abandoned by the railroad and acquired by the Whatcom County Road Department for $5000. The county used it to divert heavy logging truck traffic from a small steel structure built alongside it. In 1966 a new concrete and steel bridge was built to replace both spans and the use of the covered one was abandoned. The covered bridge fell into the river on November 12, 1972. (Deming Library)

INTERURBAN PNT (PACIFIC NORTHWEST TRACTION) CAR 80, MT. VERNON

The interurban transportation system basically had no connection to the B. B. & B. C. Railroad other than as a rail transportation alternative. It is included here to illustrate that the interurban also had major accidents. (D. Hamilton)

INTERURBAN PASSENGER CAR INTERIOR

One can see that interurban travel would be amazingly comfortable. It is assumed that they ran on very tight schedules. (D. Hamilton)

WILDCAT COVE WASHOUT, DECEMBER 13, 1924
This accident occurred someplace down on Chuckanut Drive near Larrabee
State Park on the interurban run between Bellingham and Mount Vernon.
(D. Hamilton)

WILDCAT COVE WRECKAGE
The passengers and crew barely escaped before the car slid into the washout.
(D. Hamilton)

Chapter 9
New Ownership

On September 25, 1904, death claimed the life of P. B. Cornwall, an early friend of Bellingham, in San Francisco. Mr. Cornwall had been identified with the history and growth of Bellingham Bay, as well as Seattle and San Francisco. In early days he was at the head of the Bellingham Bay Coal Company, operating coal mines in the old town of Sehome. Believing that Bellingham Bay was blessed with natural advantages bound to aid matters in the building of the city, he organized the Bellingham Bay and British Columbia Railroad Company in 1883 and began the construction of the road to connect with the Canadian Pacific in Sumas. Locally, he was an important factor in the establishment and growth of the public library, adding many books, developing Cornwall Park, and locating and building Magnolia and Dock Streets – all examples from the list of his many donations to the city.

Cornwall, who had overseen the Bellingham Bay and British Columbia and the Bellingham Bay Improvement Company as president and had taken a major interest in the fledging bay community and had retired in June 1904. Interestingly, one of the other original principal stockholders, Alvinza Hayward, had died seven months earlier.

The presidencies of the Railroad and the Improvement Company went to A. A. Taylor, a nephew of Mills.

Besides being so far from Bellingham, the new president's calculating manner contrasted sharply with the upbeat nature of Cornwall, who had been to Bellingham Bay on numerous occasions. "I don't think the plan to connect the proposed railroad to Spokane is a possibility," he wrote to Glenn C. Hyatt, land agent for the Bellingham Bay Improvement Company, in October 1905. However, Taylor added, "The agitation for the extension cannot do any harm, and one can see where it might do us considerably good."

Business people in both Bellingham and Spokane attempted to raise the necessary financing to keep the Spokane extension alive. Donovan argued with the California syndicate to participate, but the owners declined, and the effort fell short. Donovan played his last card in early 1906. He traveled to New York seeking financial backing or a buyer willing to undertake the ambitious construction project. However, a condition Mills placed on the sale of the railroad was that the real estate of the B. B. & B. C. Railroad and the Improvement Company be part of the transaction. "This package deal did not generate any enthusiasm among the easterners," wrote Beth M. Kraig in a 1981 master's degree thesis at Western Washington University titled, *A Slow Game*, the most detailed account of the California association's effort to turn

Bellingham into a major Pacific Coast city.

Taylor wrote Hyatt on March 20, 1906, complaining, "The present situation (of the B. B. & B. C.) is most unsatisfactory," adding, "There is nothing to do but to wait for developments." He recommended, "Manage the property at a minimal expense consistent with safety."

Donovan's dream never materialized, and Glacier Creek became the end of the line. According to the 1907 timetable, one passenger train per day operated each way between Glacier and Bellingham. The round trip took $3^1/_2$ hours, a travel time eventually shortened by the automobile and the more direct Mount Baker Highway.

B. B. & B. C. passenger and freight revenues, which had tripled during the first three years of the 20th century, declined after 1904. With ownership passing to the next generation, the heirs were less interested in holding onto a railroad that was not going anywhere financially. Darris Ogden Mills died on January 2, 1910, leaving his interest in the B. B. & B. C. to his daughter, Elizabeth Reid, and son, Ogden Mills. Ogden Mills was looking for a buyer.

On March 16, 1912, the entire interests of Andrew W. Rose, the D. O. Mills Estate, the P. B. Cornwall Estate and others, including all of the stock in the Bellingham Bay Improvement Company, the Bellingham Bay and British Columbia Railroad Company, the Bellingham Terminals and Railway Company, and the Bellingham Bay Lumber Company, were purchased by a syndicate of local men headed by Glen C. Hyatt, and incorporated under the name of Bellingham Securities Syndicate, Inc.

However, the sale of the local railroad companies to the Chicago, Milwaukee, and St. Paul line was officially denied at that time.

A traffic agreement was made with the latter company whereby its cars would be handled on the lines of the Bellingham Bay and British Columbia Railroad. The price for which that enormous transfer of property had been consummated was not made public.

In another announcement on March 26, 1912, by the *Bellingham Herald*:

Bellingham to get new road in year. Recent purchase of the B. B. & B. C. by Milwaukee will be followed by construction of a line from Skagit County into the city. An extension of the railroad will go into Vancouver, B.C. The road will be operated jointly by the Milwaukee and Harriman systems.

That the Chicago, Milwaukee, and St. Paul Railroad Company has purchased the Bellingham Bay and British Columbia Railroad Company and that the line will make an entry into the city from the south, along with terminals lying to the north, is now a matter of absolute certainty. Negotiations for the purchase, although only recently summarized, began about two years ago following a secret visit to the city by President Earing, who arrived here over the Great Northern Company Railroad, leaving the train at Chuckanut and coming into the city by auto. It is also a certainty that the Bellingham Terminals Railway Line will be used by the Chicago, Milwaukee, and St. Paul Company in cooperation with the Harriman System as a joint line, allowing the latter company an outlet to Vancouver, B.C., and possibly the Milwaukee Company's entrance into San Francisco.

The following day, the sale of the local railroad and stock to Milwaukee was officially confirmed by Glen C. Hyatt, President of the Bellingham Bay and British Columbia Railroad.

When the transfer was finalized and made a matter of record is not known.

On May 3 B. B. & B. C. and Glacier Coal were inspected by rail chiefs of the Milwaukee Railroad.

The Bellingham Bay and British Columbia Railroad (June 21, 1883) and the Bellingham Terminals and Railway Company (May 3, 1909) were incorporated under the general laws of California. On October 21, 1912, both entities were purchased by the Bellingham and Northern Railway Company, which had been incorporated only four days earlier on October 17, 1912, under the general laws of Washington.

With the sale, the Bellingham and Northern Railroad was composed of 66.8 miles of main track and 29 miles of yard tracks and sidings, totaling out to 95.8 miles of tracks owned and used.

The Bellingham and Northern was later sold to the Chicago, Milwaukee, and St. Paul Railroad Company on January 1, 1919. The Bellingham and Northern was a subsidiary of the Chicago, Milwaukee, and St. Paul at that time. The total connection between these two companies, and others, is extremely complicated and not known to the author.

On December 25, 1912, there was an Olympia Sale Notice of Local Merger: *Notice has been received by the Public Service Commission that the Bellingham Bay and British Columbia Railroad Company and the Bellingham Terminals Railroad Company have been absorbed by a new corporation, to be known as Bellingham and Northern Railroad Company. The merger was perfected in October but will not officially take place until January 1, 1913. The Bellingham Bay & British Columbia operates a line between Bellingham and Glacier by the way of Sumas and a branch line extending from Hampton to Lynden. The Terminals Company controls Bellingham's waterfront holdings of the Bellingham Bay and British Columbia Railroad Company, the two being operated as separate corporations. Both systems were recently purchased by the Milwaukee Railroad, and now they are being consolidated under one management.*

H.G. Selby was appointed General Agent for Milwaukee in Bellingham and arrived on January 8, 1913. Superintendent Mott Sawyer was promoted to a better position with the Milwaukee mainline, though just what it was to be was not announced. At this time Bellingham and Northern owned the line and the Chicago, Milwaukee, and St. Paul Railroad operated it.

Selby came to Bellingham from St. Louis where he had been a commercial agent for the Milwaukee. Prior to taking that position he had held a similar one for the same company in Buffalo, New York. Speaking to his work here, he said there would be no changes, at least not right away. "Everything is, I believe, operated satisfactorily. Just now I am primarily occupied in getting acquainted."

The following is a recap of the

TYPICAL CHICAGO, MILWAUKEE, AND ST. PAUL DIESEL ENGINE
With the sale of the railroad, Chicago, Milwaukee, and St. Paul started immediately replacing the old steam engines with new diesel engines. It is not known how long it took to make the total change. The old used steam engines were in some cases sold to logging railroads, but it is assumed that most of them were scrapped. (T. Schnepf)

history of the Bellingham Bay and British Columbia Railroad from its beginning to the bankruptcy of the Chicago, Milwaukee, St. Paul, and Pacific Railroad.

1. The Bellingham Bay and British Columbia Railroad was incorporated on June 21, 1883, in California.
2. It operated with standard 56$^1/_2$ inch gauge on 50/56/60-pound rail in the beginning.
3. Grading for the new track started on April 7, 1884, laying track May 6, 1884, and the first train operated on October 11, 1888, with January 31, 1904, marking the mainline's completion.
4. The carrier was placed in commercial operation on July 3, 1890.
5. The road was open to Sumas on April 1, 1891; to Maple Falls in the summer of 1901; and to Glacier in January 1904. The Lynden Branch was placed in operation on January 16, 1904, and the 11.29-mile Kulshan Line was completed in December 1916.
6. By June 30, 1891, it owned and operated 23 miles. It gradually increased to 42 miles on June 30, 1901, and 62 miles by June 30, 1909. In 1910 it had 56 miles and another 6 miles leased by the Bellingham Terminals and Railroad Company on October 1, 1909.
7. In 1909 the Chicago, Milwaukee, and St. Paul Railroad changed its name to Chicago, Milwaukee, St. Paul, and Pacific to better reflect the Pacific Coast and the Great Lakes areas.
8. On June 30, 1913, a new name was listed showing it as a 64-mile operating subsidiary of the Chicago, Milwaukee, and St. Paul Railroad Company. It was gradually extended to 80 miles by the end of December 1917, when it became a Class Two Common Carrier.
9. The Kulshan Branch's rail was removed in 1953. Part of its right of way was immediately turned over to the Washington State Highway Department to be used as part of Highway 542 to Mount Baker. Another portion of the branch was used for the construction of a county road, called the Truck Road, from Deming to below Welcome.
10. The track between Maple Falls and Glacier was taken up in 1958.
11. The track between Limestone Junction and Maple Falls was taken up in 1971.
12. The Chicago, Milwaukee, St. Paul, and Pacific Railroad went bankrupt in 1980.

Chapter 10
Railroad Memories

The fireman arrived at the roundhouse at 3 p.m. for this being a late afternoon run to Glacier with an overnight layover. Upon his arrival, the firemen reported to the little five-stall roundhouse perched on the cliff high above the tide flats and filled-in land at its foot. Originally the roundhouse had four stalls; however, a short fifth stall has been added crowding the Bellingham Bay and Eastern track which runs parallel and a little above through the alley on to the high trestle at the south end of the B. B. & B. C. Roundhouse.

Just to the west, the mainline drops at 2% to Sehome Wharf, the large mill with its extensive trackage and log dump, the waterfront yard, and the Great Northern transfer.

On this day in early summer, the 'Three' and the 'Six' are in the roundhouse. The 'One-Spot' is working at West Coast, a logging and sawmill operation west of Central, with atrocious track, old streetcar steel, antique diamond target switch stands, and no ballast. The 'Two-Spot' is on the McCush logging line out of Columbia, the 'Four' on a work train on the Mogul branch west of Clearbrook, the 'Five' on the 'Lynden Local,' trains 4, 5, 6, and 3, the 'Seven' is yard engine and pusher, and the big 'Eight' hauling a heavy log train, is storming Goshen Hill about now with "Fat" Heberden forking a ton of Carbon Hill into her white-hot firebox every eight minutes. By this time, the road has changed from wood to coal fuel.

Upon his arrival, the fireman dons his faded and patched blue overalls and jumper and starts doing the pre-trip maintenance on the locomotive. This is a process which he has done for years, including such steps as oiling various components, cleaning valves, and if time permits, some polishing of the bell.

A quick look into the firebox does show that the bank, which is the coals remaining from the previous trip which arrived back at the yard at noon, was still satisfactorily intact. With this reservoir of heat available, building up steam is good that day. The water air gauge is setting at the 90-pound mark not far from operating pressure.

About this time, Engineer Richardson arrives and starts his shift with the signing of the register. He then moves the 'Three' out of the house, over the table to the sand house, where several buckets of sand fill the sandbox. The fireman then went to work in the dead ash knocking down the bank and then deposited a shovel full or two of Puget Sound semi-lignite. After doing additional cleaning and oiling, the engineer moves the train up a 2.08% grade to the depot. A few years after this trip an entire log train was to get away here and sail down into the Bay, luckily with no loss of life.

As the train moves along, it passes

the machine and car shops where all repair work is done and much new equipment is built under the direction of a very able master mechanic. The 'rip' track parallels the 'main' on the left, and to the right are the 'middle' and 'house' tracks, making a three city block long yard gravity switching job from the top, and hard 'kicking' from the bottom, with all hand brakes clubbed.

The station on the right of the house track is a latter Victorian edifice of the boom days. It concomitantly had a hotel of the era just above it, which has ceased to function. A baggage-mail-express car and three open platform red coaches stand in front of the depot on the grade. Three express refrigerators are being placed ahead of them by the yard crew for the C. P. R. at Sumas.

After taking water, the 'Three' puffs up the grade two blocks to the three-way stub switch at Holly Street, the 'Main Street' of Bellingham, stops on the streetcar crossing and backs down to the train. It is a little after four o'clock. The fireman now has a few light chores to do, such as shoveling coal ahead and wiping the Russian iron jacket of the 'Three.' The 'Logger' comes into town with the 'Eight' at the head end.

People are passing down the platform; truckloads of baggage, and milk cans, are going through the open baggage car door. The gauge nears 140 pounds, and the three valve 'Monitor' is prime; then the fireman throws cold water into the boiler until the glass is three-quarters full. The engineer walks back to the engine, drops a little oil on the guides, and then receives the order from Conductor Kibble and the 'high sign.'

With a lever in the front corner, the throttle comes back as the train crew lets off all hand brakes, and the 'Three' 'walks' the heavy train up the grade to Holly Street, a block away. The fireman manages to pull the bell cord in intervals between several 'fires,' and gets on his seat box as the streetcar tracks are crossed, watching the horse-drawn traffic carefully. "These fool drivers, you never can tell what they'll do." A slight down grade for two blocks, with the 'Power House' siding at the right and the 'Passing Track' at the left, then around a curve to the left, and over the bridge across Whatcom Creek with a steady raising grade ahead.

The fireman firing steadily, a scoop at a time, "one to the right, one to the left, spread one under the door." On each 'fire' a glance at the stack. The exhaust is cracking like a machine gun and deepens in volume as the streetcar line is crossed again at Kentucky Street and the N. P. transfer comes alongside.

The grade increases to nearly two and three quarters percent, the exhaust blasts grow louder and slower, and we pull up Iron Street and through a long curve up to the doubling siding at Summit, high above Bellingham.

The bar comes back to three or four notches from the center, and the throttle goes in to ease up the pressure on the balanced slide valves to the optimum running condition. We curve to the right down a two percent grade to Squalicum 'bottom,' crossing the creek. In a few years, the mainline will branch off here and go down the creek to the north end of the Bay, and the hill we have just come over will not be crossed by rails above Pride's Cannery.

A one and one-half pull takes us up through Dewey, and we level off through Van Wyck Station, named after the firemen's father. Stopping here, we unload milk cans and many passengers who have done their shopping in Bellingham between trains. Then by 'Noon Number One' and 'Two,' sawmill spurs, and then up the sharp pitch of Cougar Hill, better than one percent, passing the spot where the 'Six' dropped her crown sheet the previous fall. We stop at Wahl, where a country road leads off to prosperous farms and cutover lands.

Next, we come to the top of Goshen Hill. Two percent and better, it drops down to Goshen Flat, and then down another steep pitch and through a double reverse curve above the Nooksack River. Several years later, the Kulshan branch will be a built from here. Through Welcome and up the Middle Fork of the Nooksack, heavy log trains will originate in this area from the logging railways of the St. Paul and Tacoma Lumber Company.

A calf gets on the track and pays no attention to the 'cattle alarm.' The engine slows down and the fireman runs out along the running board, down the 'long nosed' pilot, off the angle iron step, and chases the calf, who chooses to remain on the track until he reaches the cattle guard at the foot of the hill. A badly winded fireman 'flips' the high step and climbs back into the cab, to buckle down to steady shoveling as the 'Three' gets back on schedule.

No passengers for Central today and the 'Local' is late, to be met up the line. The 'West Coast' logging line stretches away to the west. We pass Millerton, a lonely sidetrack, with nothing left to show that it was a busy terminal in 1891 with stage service to the Nooksack Ferry and on to the Boundary.

Strandell comes into view, with 'Engine Five' and 'Train Six' mixed, in the siding. Here we cross the 'Nordstrom' railroad, a logging line of some seven feet gauge, operated by a homemade locomotive which stands on the log deck of the Nordstrom mill. It is a 2-2-0, a two-drum logging 'donkey,' with chain drive to a pair of spoked pony truck wheels, which originally belonged to 'Engine Four.' A sprocket on the haul back drum gives a 'high' speed with the empties. The 'tender' is a flat car with a peaked roof to keep the wood dry.

After doing our station work, we pull the grade up to the long drawbridge over the wide Nooksack River. Years back sternwheelers came up here and beyond. We passed the water tank and stop at Everson, a busy town with farms and shingle mills. Then comes Hampton where the Lynden branch runs due west down through the rich alluvial Nooksack bottom land to the busy farming and mill town of Lynden. We pause briefly, and then roar away through Van Buren to Clearbrook, stopping to fill the tank as the hills have taken a heavy toll of coal and water.

A wooden rail tramway used to run to Northwood Mill west of here, said to have been worked by a box-cab engine, possibly a Climax or old Porter dummy. Mogul Spur branches off a little to the north and runs into big timber. Every train of logs originates here from along the boundary. We see the afternoon N. P. passenger train across the fields to the east as we race on to Sumas over level country, passing Haverstick Spur, another logging operation. At a road crossing, we hit some 40-pound ex-streetcar steel where a little later this fireman and Lon Hunt are to hit a cow with 'Engine Four' on a Sunday passenger run and go in the ditch.

Here we head in the west leg of the 'wye' and back down to Sumas, taking several ton buckets of coal in the move, and stop at the platform for Customs inspection. We then back across the border to Huntington, B.C.

After an hour in these busy surroundings with Sumas Prairie stretching back to the snow-covered peaks in front of us, we get the highball for the finish of our trip. With the headlight burning, we pull out through the east leg of the 'wye' past busy saw and shingle mills, through Lamberton to the entrance of Saar Creek Canyon and the start of the 'Big Hill.' For four miles the grade will vary from three to three and one-quarter percent. The exhaust echoes from the steep canyon walls. If it were full daylight and the fireman were not shoveling coal steadily, an unparalleled scenic view would be his to behold. A rumble tells him that Bridge Four, in itself a noteworthy scenic attraction, is being crossed. The cab rolls to the right and left in the sharp reverse curves of the canyon. Finally, Hill Top and Columbia are reached; the fireman can catch a breath of cool mountain air from the gangway.

At Columbia, the McCush logging railway branches off. Then comes Kendall, a busy town, near which a heavy load limestone industry will spring up later. Now the bar drops down for the 'two point two' into Maple Falls, a busy logging town. The bridge over the Nooksack shows up in the headlight's yellow beam as water is taken, then we pound steadily along

the roaring Nooksack River, cold and milky from its glaciers high up to the northeast, to Glacier.

At Glacier, the turntable and one small engine shed is passed, and 'Number One' pulls up alongside the station platform with the 'Three's' pilot near the end of the track, above Glacier Creek. This is the terminus. None of the grandiose dreams of the boom days of building to Okanogan Valley and on to Spokane, ever materialized. When we leave on 'Number Two' at 7 a.m., the pack trains with horseback loads of goods for the mines, secured by expertly thrown diamond hitches, will be leaving in the opposite direction up the steep canyon trails, past the Nooksack power plant, past Mount Shuksan and Mount Baker, for the dim and little-known interior of Whatcom County, the high backbone of the Cascades.

These excerpts are mainly edited segments of what a fireman might have seen during a trip from Bellingham to Glacier aboard Engine #3 in 1906, reprinted from *The Railway and Locomotive Historical Society, Inc., Bulletin No. 84*, printed in 1951.

Here in my 14th summer, 1919, I had my first well-paying job. I dried sand for the logging locomotive. The Church Mountain track grade was steep. The train stopped and filled the sand dome on top of the engine nearly every trip on rainy days. Without sand on the tracks in front of the driving wheels, the wheels slipped, and the train came to a halt. The engineer pulled the cord to open a little pipe about an inch in front of the wheels and then the sand trickled out onto the tracks.

My job was to dry out sand that did

give the locomotive traction it needed. In a ditch beside the track beyond the camp was a handy sand and gravel bank. This was the spot where I set up my camp to dry the sand. I first screened up the gravel, then by shoveling the sand on top of a 4'x 8' steel sheet and keeping the fire going under it, the sand was dried. I cut my own wood from logs which were rolled off the train for me. There was a canvas fly to pull over the top on rainy days. There was so much steam sometimes that I seemed to be just boiling water. Had to be careful of the fly not to burn it. Had to be careful also not to let a lingering fire start a forest fire. There were several 50-gallon drums on hand of dry sand. They lasted one locomotive a few days.

McRea

As a young teenager living with my parents at the base of Red Mountain where the O. P. C. Rock Loading Facility was located, it was an ideal spot for adventures. On the Sumas-Kendall Road, this was referred to as Limestone Junction. With the help of my two cousins who lived just above Kendall, we had great days of exploring.

Now at this location there is an exceptionally large concrete silo where the rock is stored in preparation for loading. The railroad cars go directly under the structure and are backed uphill on the grade. Now one of the great things when we were venturing about was checking out the railroad cars. The first few cars in the row were already loaded with rock and maybe another dozen behind in preparation. Now each one of these railroad cars had a handbrake on it which was a steel rotating wheel, and we would love to play with those brakes. We went all the way down to the lower end and one of the cousins decided to play with a hand wheel and in doing so the whole line of cars started rolling down the tracks with one or more of us on the railroad, and we all started turning the wheels to re-apply the brake. After all of us jumped clear, we watched the cars gain speed.

We finally got the train cars stopped and I would assume that was the only string of cars that went into Bellingham to be unloaded and in the middle there were two or three cars without a rock.

SAND DRYING STOVE

For Railroads, Trolley Lines, Contractors, Coal Companies, Etc.

INDIANA FOUNDRY CO.

Code: FILIAL

The above is a cut of the complete Sand Drier. The wet sand is shoveled into the skirting and, as it dries, will of itself run through the holes in the ring at the bottom of the skirting. The amount of sand the stove will dry depends on how wet the sand is and on the condition of the fire in the stove. The stove may be fed with hard or soft coal, coke or wood. Clear sand only can be used. Earth or clay would bake hard and fail to run through holes in the ring. Always have a good fire in the stove before the sand is put in, otherwise the sand may bake and not discharge itself.

No. 2—Capacity about 5 tons daily and weighs about 700 lbs.

Price $70.00

Prices Approximately Net and Subject to Market Changes

PAGE 294   Contractors Equipment Co. PORTLAND SEATTLE

SAND DRYING STOVE
McRea probably did not even have the knowledge that a piece of modern equipment was available for sand drying. (Contractors Equipment Company)

Once again living with my parents, this time we lived at a company camp for Clawson Limestone Company. Across the highway was the railroad spur and facility for loading the rock. One year a man lived in a railroad caboose all summer. The railroad company had brought in a large D8 bulldozer and taken it down on the river. That man and that bulldozer spent the whole summer down there in attempting to channel the river to the far side. As I recall, the first big flood and it was back on the original side of the Nooksack.
Dennis Jenkins

The Catholic Church for the area was located on the Sumas-Kendall Road in the area of the Limestone Junction Road. Each summer all the local Catholic kids were sent to this church for catechism classes and directly across from the church were the B. B. & B. C. Railroad tracks. Our instructors must have known at approximately what time the train would be going by, and we would have a recess.

Now the big thing for the boys was to cross the road and be as near to the train as possible. But a big thing each day was to put coins on the track and allow the train to flatten them. Now I enjoyed this because that coin would be as flat as a sheet of paper, but I never used anything bigger than a nickel.

One of my biggest adventures with the railroad occurred with myself and three other boys. I am not sure that I was the youngest of the group but let us assume that I was. We had decided to ride our bicycles up to Maple Falls from Kendall to investigate the 80-foot-high trestle of the railroad which was located right on the edge of town. I am sure that none of our parents knew of our venture and the fact that we were going to ride our bikes three miles up the crooked Mount Baker Highway where hundreds of logging trucks were traveling.

Upon reaching the bridge and dumping our bicycles in the brush, we decided to venture out on the bridge. At about the three-quarter point of crossing the bridge, one of the older boys identified the sound of the train coming down from Glacier. Train or no train, I must admit that I was terribly scared to be on the bridge at all.

The deck on the bridge for walking was the ties spaced apart and then on the outside one continuous 2 x 12. Now us boys not being mature men, if you missed your step your foot would be between the ties, so we were forced to walk on the single 2 x 12.

Now at a point that the group was almost being off the bridge, the train was now on the bridge on the far end. The leader of our group said we could not make it back and gave the command to climb down on the timbers under the track and wait for the train to pass over us. So, in fact that is what we did, with me and one of the other immature little kids sitting below crying our eyes out. We can feel the bridge shaking as the train came forward and then stopped. The engine stopped directly above us and was setting there with hot water dripping off it, splattering down on us. After what seemed like a lifetime, the train started to continue its trip; and with what seemed like hours it was gone, and we then climbed back up and got off the bridge. What we did not realize, we were only about 15 feet from being off the bridge as it was.

We then loaded ourselves on the

bicycles and went like hell back to Kendall.

Remember the movie 'STAND BY ME.'

Michael Impero

I got a worker permit for the summer of 1953, when I was 17 years old, to work summers for the railroad. My older brother Richard was already working for the railroad. Currently, my pay was $1.50 per hour and we started work at 7 a.m. with a half hour lunch break and off at 3:30 p.m. Ed Cave was my boss and he was the section boss from Limestone Junction to Glacier. Our starting point each morning was Maple Falls.

There was a total of four men in our work crew with me being one of them. Our working vehicle was called a motor car or speeder. Attached to that would be a two-axle wagon behind, which would haul all the tools and materials. We would start out of a building in Maple Falls. The four men would ride on the motorcar which propelled himself along the railroad.

We had a variety of projects which we performed. Our main function was replacing damaged railroad ties. With the constant threat of fires started by a locomotive, we were constantly on fire control. Under all the bridges we would clear out any brush to the side and burn it. Any bark falling off from logs on a logging train, leaves etc. that accumulated on the tracks, we also would rake aside.

When we were busy clearing brush, Ed would take the motor car and travel up the track inspecting the ties and marking the ones that needed to be replaced. The replacing of a railroad tie started with the removal of approximately 25 feet of tie spikes each side of the rejected one. These sections of this rail could be extremely heavy with the rail up to 65-pound rail. Removing came next and would be with railroad bars lifting the rail above the tie and then sliding the tie out. This was extremely physical, and a new tie was be replaced and drawn up proper. And then tamping ballast rock around. When this was complete all the railroad spikes would be replaced. If it was a high replacement day, the crew had a quantity of ties that were required to be completed. The crew had some type of device that they placed each day at their work zone to indicate to the train crew of their work in the area. Also, in conjunction with the ties, at times the crew would be required to put in the switching mechanism for a new spur to be added.

Another function that was required on almost a daily basis was to investigate all the ditches and culverts to see if there is any blockage by nature or by beavers. Also, on each bridge there were firefighting water barrels and our job was to confirm that the barrels were full of water, and if not, to add water.

In my second year working for the railroad I did the same type work starting at 7 a.m. and was through at 3:30 p.m. Then I went to a mill in Maple Falls and worked from 4 p.m. to 12 a.m. each day. The following year I worked only for the sawmill, higher pay.

Robert Joyce

I am 68 years old and went to and graduated from Meridian High School. I became a schoolteacher and I taught at Nooksack Valley High School for 39 years, that being my only teaching job. Worked for the railroad in the summertime when going to college. The name of the railroad at that time was Chicago, Milwaukee, St. Paul, and Pacific. My job for the railroad was from 1970 to 1976 with one summer off. The last year that I knew that it operated was the year that the railroad bridge in Everson burned down. Rumor has it that a couple of teenage boys started the fire.

I worked for the railroad for either four or five years. The year that I graduated I went back working for that summer. By the time that I worked for the railroad all the steam locomotives were gone and diesel had replaced them. I worked with the Sumas Section Crew. However, one summer I worked on what was called a gang crew which worked on the full length of the track.

Yes, I do remember structures in Sumas. One being the main depot and the other being the Sumas Section Crew Building which housed our motor car and all of our tools. This was the location where we reported to work each morning. Our shift went from I believe 7:30 a.m. to 4:00 p.m., five days a week. This building was located about half a mile south of the main depot. We got two 15-minute breaks per day and half an hour for lunch.

Each morning the section foreman would go to the main depot and meet with an agent right at the border and get the work order for that particular day and get a copy of the safety rules that came from Milwaukee by a telegram, printed out, that pertained to this particular day. The foreman would read this to the crew before leaving

Sumas. He also gave an initial report of the assignment of work for that particular day to the four-man crew. A fellow by the name of Shepley would come up occasionally from Seattle, make an inspection of a section of track, and then identify to us what needed to be done.

Yes, the train would go into Canada and pick up cars or deliver cars. At the time that I was working for the railroad, there were actually two trains operating each day. One train's total responsibility was delivering empty cars to the limestone quarry and then return with a full strength of cars with limestone rock to the cement plant in Bellingham. The other train was strictly a freight train and it went to obviously Sumas, then went as far as Limestone Junction and Lynden. The main function of this train was to move freight. At times, the limestone train would also move freight if needed.

Our railroad boss was, I believe, a fellow by the name of Roland and he lived right in Sumas near the depot and as far as I know he owned his own home.

I think that the decision on the scope of the work for the day was actually a joint thing between him and the man at the depot. Also, it depended on the different times of the year.

In late spring every year, we would brush out the railroad right of way, particularly under the bridges. Another thing that was done every year at this time was the removal any new brush from the visual triangular shaped land at railroad crossings. The idea was that as a vehicle approached a railroad crossing it could look down the railroad and observe if any train were coming.

The Milwaukee had a formula of about 15° that was used and occasionally we actually measured out this triangular piece of land. The long leg of this triangle was approximately 250 feet. The brush was removed for basically two reasons: first being potential of a fire and a second strictly for visibility. Another thing that was seasonal, and this applied to wintertime, we chipped out the ice from a railroad crossing so that the train would not derail because of the ice buildup.

By the time that I was working there were only two section crews when earlier there would have been many more. The Bellingham crew went from the start of the railroad in Bellingham out to the Van Wyck Road. Now that does not seem like a tremendous large area but in Bellingham and around the depot there were a lot of maintenance crossings to be taken care of. Our zone was from Limestone Junction to the north side of the Van Wyck. At the time, there was still track leading to Maple Falls, but it was becoming an abandoned state. At the Limestone Junction, the engine of the train was turned around.

The cement plant, to the best of my knowledge, owned their spur going in off the Sumas-Kendall Road to the quarry face. We traveled on their track a short distance in switching the cars, but I do not recall going all the way into the quarry or to Kendall.

I worked for a subcontractor on weekends one summer and he had a contract to run a spur into the substation in Dewey Valley. And because we were working for the substation, I am positive that the substation paid for the spur.

All tools were short-handled tools, with picks, mauls, and shovels being square point. Our line crews had no mechanical equipment of any kind, and we would look over at the Burlington Northern with all modern equipment, tamping machines, spiking machines, etc. All the Milwaukee locomotives and cars were bought into Bellingham on barges and unloaded down on the water in front of Haley International. Yes, the barge loading facility was still at the end of Cornwall Avenue and they had about five or six tracks leading off the dock which were used for loading and unloading off barges. Yes, they had like a ferry type ramp that was used for the loading and unloading.

Every morning before the work was to commence the foreman or the boss had a standard saying that he would repeat, "I want to see nothing but ass holes and elbows." And yes, you were bent over all day with all the short-handled tools. Of the three normal occupations of the area, logging was considered to be the most dangerous, with mining and railroading to follow. But the railroads were really quite safe and every morning without fail the safety report was read to us. At the time of my work, we definitely had "social distancing." All of us were swinging mauls or using 6-foot-long pry bars and other tools, you had to stay away from each other. We rode to work from Sumas each day on a little motorized car called a "motor car" with a four-cylinder motor. It had a windshield with a top and side curtains along the sides that rolled down or rolled up. These curtains were made from some kind of clear plastic. However, they obviously had not been cleaned in years. In the motor car there was room for two people on each side and you faced to the outside. The motor transmission was situated between the two benches in the center and in the wintertime it produced a very comfortable heat. This motor car could reach a speed of about 35 mph. The operator sat on the corner of one of the two benches so he could have reasonable visibility and he had a throttle and a long-handled brake. The motor car had a forward gear and reverse gear. However, the car had to be completely stopped before shifting. When we needed to change direction, the four of us would stop the car at a siding. There were some steel bars on the car; two at the front and two at the back that slid out, and the four of us would pick this machine and move it off the main track. When we were straightening track, we would get what is called lining bars. We would slide these bars under the rail and then the foreman would holler "1, 2, 3, heave." We worked together and each time we put the "1, 2, 3, heave" to it, it would only move about one inch. But it was remarkable how we could move it and, in some cases, we moved the ties and the rail completely together. One of the factors that caused misalignment of the rails was summer heat and the expansion. We had no means to solve this problem.

We towed behind the yellow motor car a little wagon called 'push car,' dirty gray in color. We could tow one of these behind us, have all our tools and a pile of ties aboard, going to a place of work that day. Or you could hook two together to haul railroad rails and they would act as a reach similar to a logging truck. This would place the

TYPICAL B. B. & B. C. MOTOR CAR
This is one of many different styles of motor cars. They came in a variety of capacities for carrying the workers and weather protection for the crew. It is not known how many this railroad had, but every section crew would have had one or two. (Internet)

'push cars' about 33 feet apart.

If it were determined to be the fire season the foreman would go into Bellingham and follow the train out to watch for fires. When he went to Bellingham, he would pick up a smaller motor car with water cans aboard and followed the train out and back observing for possible fires.

The normal for placing ties was ten ties per day per man. The boss would come around driving a pickup to check on our work. I believe that we worked with 80 to 90-pound rail. That is measured in weight per three feet or per yard. The wear on the sides of the rail on a curve varied from the outside to the inside. At times, we would take up the two rails and switch them to get equal wear. Yes, on corners there was a camber built into the outside track and there was a tool for measuring it. They had a bar that had a level

STANDARD CUTTER MATTOCKS

Fig. 758-A

BLACK JAPAN FINISH—POLISHED BEVELS

Weight, each	Lbs.	5	6
Price	Per doz.	$16.00	$17.00
Width of blade	Ins.	2½, 3 & 3½	3 & 4
Length of cutter	"	4¾	5¼

RAILROAD AND CARPENTER'S ADZES

Fig. 758-B

RAILROAD ADZE, PICK EYE

Fig. 758-C

CARPENTER'S ADZE, HALF HEAD

Solid steel, hammer forged, ground smooth, well tempered. Black baked dull rubber finish.

		Railroad	Carpenter's
Kind of adze		Railroad	Carpenter's
Price	Per doz.	$24.00	$24.00
Weight, each (average)	Lbs.	5½	4
Length, overall	Ins.	11	9
Width of blade	"	5	3½ to 4½

Adze handles shown on page 757.

RAILROAD TRACK CHISELS

Fig. 758-D

Size of body (square)	Inches	1⅝
Price	Each	$2.10
Weight	Pounds	5
Curved bit	Inches	1¼
Length	"	8½

BELL PATTERN RAILROAD SPIKE MAULS

Fig. 758-E

Weight	Pounds	10
Price	Each	$1.90
Length	Inches	15¼
Diameter face	"	1¼

CARPENTER'S WRECKING BARS

Fig. 758-F

GOOSE NECK PATTERN

Fig. 758-G

LEETONIA

STRAIGHT PATTERN

Both ends are tempered. Polished finish claw chisel, black finish body.

		Goose Neck	
Pattern		Goose Neck	
Price	Per dozen	$7.20	$6.00
Weight, per dozen	Pounds	61	42
Length	Inches	36	24
Diameter octagon steel.	"	¾	¾

PINCH POINT CROW BARS

Fig. 758-H

Size	Inches	1	1¼
Price	Each	$1.25	$1.60
Weight, each	Pounds	10	14
Length	Feet	4	4½

WEDGE POINT CROW BARS

Fig. 758-I

Size	Inches	1¼
Price	Each	$1.60
Weight, each	Pounds	14
Length	Feet	4½

DIAMOND POINT LINING BARS

Fig. 758-J

Size	Inch	
Price	Each	
Weight	Pounds	
Length	Feet	

CLAW BARS

WITH HEEL AND CHISEL END

Fig. 758-K

Length	Feet	
Price	Each	
Weight, each	Pounds	

GOOSE NECK CLAW BARS

Fig. 758-L

Weight	Pounds	
Price	Each	

TRACK WRENCHES

Fig. 758-M

Size of bolt	Inches	⅞
Price	Each	$1.40
Size of opening	Inches	1½
Length	"	20
Weight, each	Pounds	4

MISCELLANOUS SECTION CREW TOOLS, PAGE #1
This page illustrates a variety of tools that would have been used by the section line crew. Some of the tools are not complete as shown such as the maul, chisels, and others as they are lacking their handles. (Hendrie Bolthoff Catalog, p. 758)

TAMPING BARS

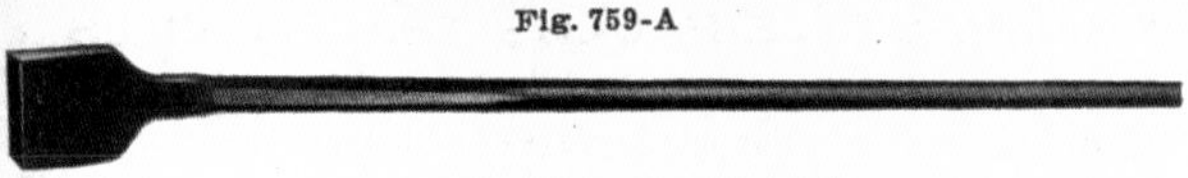

Fig. 759-A

Length, 5½ feet. Approximate weight, 14 pounds.
Price, each..... **$2.60**

RAIL FORKS

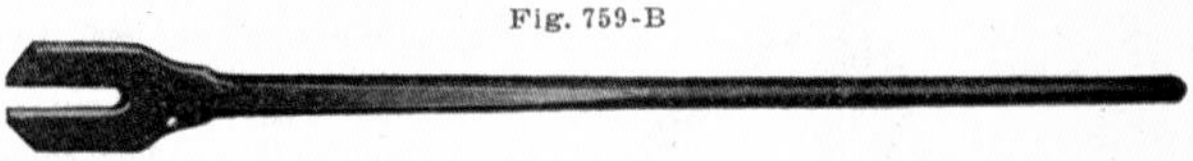

Fig. 759-B

Approximate weight, 25 pounds.
Price, each..... **$3.00**

RAIL TONGS

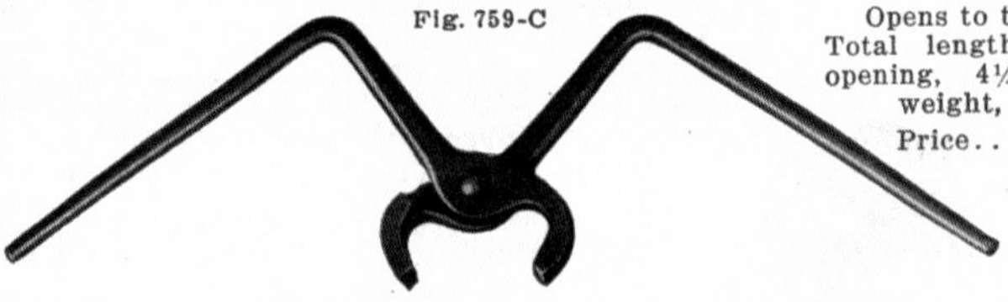

Fig. 759-C

Opens to take a 6-inch girder rail. Total length, 39 inches; greatest opening, 4¼ inches; approximate weight, 18 pounds.
Price............Each **$4.00**

SAMSON CAR AND LOCOMOTIVE MOVERS

Made of malleable iron and crucible tool steel, except the handle, which is of second-growth hard maple.

		Car	Locomotive
Price	Each	$8.00	$9.00
Weight	Pounds	16	21
Extreme length	Inches	68	71

CAR MOVER EXTRA PARTS

No.		Price, Each
0	Cam	$0.50
2	Wood Handle	2.00
3	Square Spur, $\frac{9}{16}$x 3-inch	.50
9	Triangular Spur, $\frac{11}{16}$x3-inch	.50
4	Spring	.50
5*	Channel Arm with Cam	3.00
6	Shoe for Triangular Spur	2.00
8	Shoe for Square Spur	2.00
11	Clamp	.40
27*	Socket Arm with Cam or Toggle	3.00
A	Clamp Bolt	.10
B	Shoe Bolt	.10
C	Shoe Rivet	.10
D	Cam Pin	.10
R	Arm and Handle Bolt	.10

LOCOMOTIVE MOVER EXTRA PARTS

No.		Price, Each
10	Cam	$0.50
11	Clamp	.40
12	Handle	2.25
13	One-piece Spur ($\frac{9}{16}$ square)	.50
14	Spring	.50
15	Channel Arm with Cam or Toggle	3.25
16	Shoe	2.25
J	Clamp Bolt, $\frac{7}{16}$x 1¼	.10
K	Shoe and Arm Bolt, ½x2¾	.10
L	Shoe Rivet, $\frac{7}{16}$x 1¾	.10
M	Cam Pin, ½x2	.10
S	Arm and Handle Bolt	.10

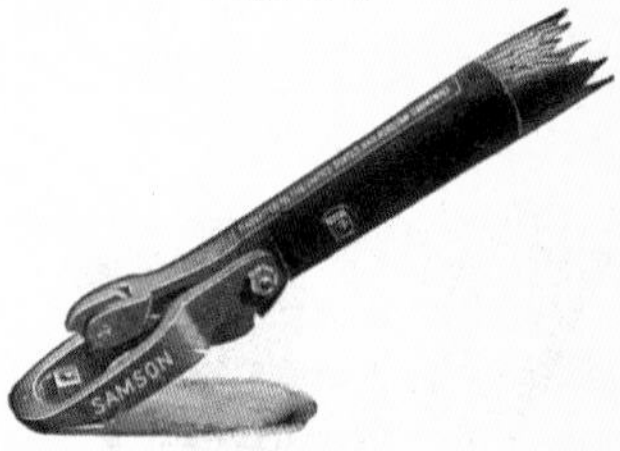

Fig. 759-D

Care should be exercised when ordering spurs, to state definitely whether they shall be square or triangular, as a square spur will not fit a shoe made for a triangular spur.
***When ordering, specify whether channel arm or socket arm.**

ROWELL ROCKER BEARING CAR MOVERS

The two big outstanding factors of the Rowell are its tremendous forward thrust and its powerful rotating leverage. It is the proper functioning of these two important factors at all angles and under all positions on the rail that makes the Rowell the nearest to a switch engine for spotting cars of any man-power appliance known. A maximum thrust is provided by the Rowell cam and lever principle, and quick follow-up is facilitated by the strong steel spring which lifts the spur instantly from the rail and also protects it from wear and breakage.

Price	Each	$10.00
Weight	Pounds	20
Extreme length	Inches	68

EXTRA PARTS

No.		Price, Each
0	Cam or Toggle	$0.50
R- 5	Upper Shoe Casting with Steel Toe Rivet	2.00
R- 6	Spur Plate or Clamp	.50
R- 7	Lower Shoe Casting	1.00
R- 8	Tool Steel Spurs (per set of 2 pieces)	.50
R- 9	Bolt for Socket Arm	.10
R-10	Steel Rivet for Cam No. 0	.10
R-11	Steel Toe Rivet for Shoe No. R-5	.10
R-12	Bolt for Spur Plate No. R-6	.10
R-13	Rock Maple Handle	2.00
27	Socket Arm Casting complete, with Cam or Toggle attached	3.00

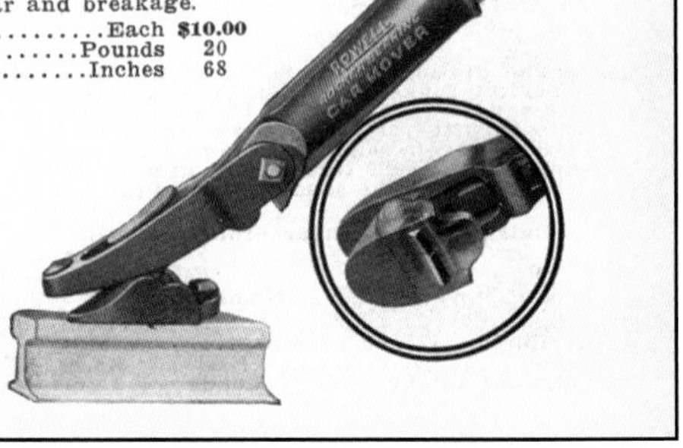

Fig. 759-E

MISCELLANEOUS SECTION CREW TOOLS, PAGE #2
(Hendrie Bolthoff Catalog, p. 759)

ELDERLY MAN MOVING A FULLY LOADED RAILROAD CAR
This simple hand tool had the capacity as stated and shown to move a railroad car. This device moved the car approximately one inch each time it was levered. The car mover was used for a truly short distance. (Internet)

attached, and with a printed chart you could determine how much higher the outside rail had to be. The boss was never a working hand. The foreman was a working man, but not the boss man. When we were working on the radius of a curve he would come and determine the elevation of the outside rail. There was a boss, a foreman, and two worker bees. I worked in the summer replacing workers as they were taking their vacations.

The reason I got hired by the railroad in the summer was because the farmer that I worked for was an engineer on the railroad. He praised my

work habits, particularly in shoveling manure. His recommendation is what got me hired. Two days after graduating from high school I was working on the Milwaukee Railroad.

One of the first days of my employment, we were replacing rail and the spike maul was the hammer that drove in the railroad spikes. It had a very narrow head on it and quite long. It was made this way so that you could actually drive the spike from over the other side of the rail and if you missed the spike you would not break the head off. I remember going to the toolbox and getting out a spike maul and carrying to

SAMSON CAR MOVERS

The Samson Car Mover was a marvelous tool which could move a railroad car with only six-foot leverage on the handle. In the early 1900s it sold for $5.50. (E. Erickson)

the work area. I was told by one of the workers that that maul is John's maul. I then replied, being a young "smart alec," I do not see no name on it other than Milwaukee. No, that is John's and it will work by itself. Actually, it was not long before I broke the handle of a hammer and then I was taught how to hang a head. When you are driving spikes, I was told, let the hammer do the work. Driving spikes was not like splitting wood as you kept your two hands together on the handle and created a round house swing.

The procedure of replacing a tie was that first you did not jack up the rail because you did not want some of the ballasts falling under the adjoining ties.

You would dig out alongside the tie that you were about to replace, then you would grab a hold of the end of the tie using tie tongs and pull it out to either the right or the left. You normally would work on one tie only, but you could do three or four at a time in a row. The boss would come by and he would either mark the ties with some kind of paint marking or chalk on the rails, so we knew the tie to be replaced. All the members of the crew, other than myself, were older than 50 years old. One of the members of the crew was nicknamed "High Ball Harry," the foreman. One particular day, we had 33 ties on the pushcart. Our work area that day was between Everson and Hampton. Under a hot, burning sun, we put in the 33 ties, straightened five links of rail, and tamped it back into usable condition.

From Hampton to Lynden there was hardly a roadbed. Yes, this roadbed totally lacked proper construction. A lot of it was through beautiful farmlands and other parts through bog type land. They never took the rock train in on this section; and if they had some cars connected to the rock cars, they would be left out at Hampton. There at the Hampton station it was quite common that the train would unload or load farming materials.

I have a story about Big John Postma who was a Lynden farmer. John would wear them overalls every day and occasionally those straps would fall down over his shoulder, and he would be forced to take a break. I do not know if he liked taking a break, or if he was just too tired. At one point, John and I were the total crew and we were assigned the work completing respiking on a section of rail near the Sumas asphalt shingle business. I believe that the two of us went through 5 gallons water in one day. The two of us spent four days, hot summer days, doing nothing but spiking those rails down. I really admired how hard he could work; he was over 60 and I was 19. He retired a few years later and then one winter day he was helping a neighbor push out a car stopped in a snowbank and had a heart attack and died.

Think that I will now talk about Saar Creek Canyon which is up near Cedar Springs today. This was the most rugged construction area in the whole line and the steepest grade of the railroad. In this canyon area there were three timber trestle bridges and another which was a combination of a wood trestle and a fabricated steel bridge. We did not do any maintenance or repair work on the bridges. That work was performed by a separate railroad bridge crew. They brought their own special cars and lived in Pullman cars in Sumas. The brushing out in the right of way and below these bridges was performed by the section line crew. We would cut an assortment of trees, blackberries, skunk cabbage and anything that grew under the bridge. We used hook axes, scythes, normal axes, and cross-cut saws. The work that I performed on the railroad was most enjoyable, but the area up in the Canyon was the most scenic and most beautiful with that flowing stream directly below us. I carried in those days the normal lunch pail with a rounded top and each day that lunch pail was crammed to the top with sandwiches and trust me, I ate them all. It would take me the total half hour lunch just to eat all the sandwiches. Sometimes when the boss was not

around and the sun shining, we would take a little nap.

At the end of each bridge there was a platform constructed and a 55-gallon wood barrel was set there and was full of water. Water was there to combat any fire that that may start near the bridge; but in my years, I never saw any fire. It got to be great enjoyment for kids to come up and tip the barrel over the side and watch the barrel and the water rushing away. So, the railroad decided at the end of the bridge to dig a hole and bury the barrel full of water with a wood lid and maybe have three or four inches above grade. Well, over a period the location of the barrels was completely hidden by a layer of vegetation. I was working along the end of the railroad at a bridge, stepped right into one of these barrels with one foot with the lid collapsing, and in went - one leg inside the barrel and one leg outside the barrel. The barrel was taller than the length of my leg so we can visualize what occurred when the rim of the barrel made contact between my legs. All the older men got a real big charge out of this.

When the temperature in the summertime got so high, they had to put on fire watch. And it was the responsibility of the boss to go to town and to get an extra motor car and survey behind the train going and coming. Occasionally he got off the motor car and started a small fire. He would then report this in the daily report, and it was decided it was necessary to continue the fire watch.

Each morning the Bellingham Station would put out a daily schedule for the trains, and this would show the approximate time that they would be at each location.

The approximate time that the train would arrive at our location where we were doing a project, we were required to place torpedoes on the track. These torpedoes were a sequence of markings that we put on the railing to slow down the train. You were not supposed to hold up the train or to make the train stop. You were required to have all your work completed and the railroad track open when the train came. We always put out torpedoes as required.

Under one of the trestles we discovered an entrance to a clay mine and we went in exploring, but not far, because we did not have any form of light.

We were returning from work in the motor car with two push cars loaded with rail and it was an extremely hot day and with the added heat of the motor on the motor car. All of us on the motorcar fell asleep. Now any time that the train approached a road crossing, the train had the right of way at the crossing; however, for the motor car this was not similar. As a motor car approached the crossing it did not have the right of way and was required to stop. Well, one day as I said earlier, we all had fallen asleep, and suddenly, we heard blasting of a horn which woke us up immediately. We realized we were at Mission Road Crossing and, of course, we were not stopping and there was a

RAILROAD TORPEDO ALARM

The torpedo alarm was a device that was attached to the top of the rail. As a railroad engine, or any other type of device riding on the rails, rolled over it, an explosion would be set off. The section line crew automatically were required to install the alarm in an area in which they were working. This was strictly a safety device, and upon the completion of the work for the day they removed it for reuse at another time. (M. Impero)

car approaching with blazing horn. All three of us lunged for the brake and I saw smoke from the car tires. Thinking that the car was going to hit us directly in the side, I expected a full collision; so, I was the only one that jumped off the car and rolled down the bank. They did not hit us and kept going. The remaining members of the crew car stopped and were all in a state of shock. We all had the vision of our lives passing in front of us. This was the last day of work for me that summer and I sure could have went out in a blaze of glory.

The Milwaukee Road was noted for their creative ingenuity in making makeshift equipment. Well, it really was not to Milwaukee's credit, it was the farm boys that created a lot of the improvements. As I said, the Milwaukee was a very tight run operation for what reason I am not sure. One of the ideas was the concept of making a mowing machine that would eliminate all the hand scything work on both sides of the rail. We took a typical, for the day, old horse drawn mowing machine which had a steel seat, a lever that would raise the mower cutter bar, and another lever that would throw it out of gear. There was no kick out mechanism if the operator hit something to release the bar. And if you did hit something you were to derail the machine. This machine had railroad wheels placed on it and it was towed by the motor car. A safety precaution that the farm boys created was instead of having a steel pin connecting the mower to the motor car, they use a pin made from vine maple. If the cutter bar hit something solid, it would lift the machine off the rails and then you would be going down

on top of the ties. Operating the mowing machine, I was approximately five to six feet behind the motor car.

One summer I was on a special crew headed up by "Highball Harry." The order for the special crew came direct from Milwaukee and it had between 15 and 16 men. It was probably as close to a prison gang crew that one can imagine. They gave us a tamper and tie cutter. We also had a machine that helped get the ties in place. We met right where the work had ended the day before so there is no riding in the motor car and there was also no reading of the Milwaukee Safety Rules each day. This crew averaged well above ten ties per man per day. The reason this work was being done was because the overall condition of the whole line of the rails and the ties was deteriorating so quickly that the railroad had to take a major step. We were almost completely back to Bellingham when we got the official word that the funding for the project had been used up and today was the last day. The boss went at the end of the day and got a case of beer, and we all sat along the railroad shoulder and drank one beer.

Yes, I was in the railroad union. I did not get health benefits because I was not a full-time employee. I paid in union dues monthly, but I did not have to pay in my share of Social Security. The railroad had its own Social Security system and unemployment program. The one summer that I did not get hired, I signed up for the program and got it at the same time I was going to college. Now, if I would have gotten dispatched to a job, I would have had to drop out of my college courses. When I filled out the unemployment forms, I went to the

Milwaukee office on Railroad Avenue. I believe today that little brick building is a pizza joint.

I got hurt one time. We were at a new road crossing replacing some of the material. I was driving spikes at that location and suddenly, a big gob of sawdust and creosote flew up into my eye. I went to a nearby house and they put Vaseline in the eye with the creosote and in no time flat it solved the problem.

I really appreciated the time I worked with these true old-timers that had marvelous work ethics and personally it gave me a lot of direction for the rest of my life.
Rod McKissick

MAINLINE SQUALICUM SPLIT
This is the mainline split at the south end of Dewey Valley at the location where the railroad crossed Squalicum Creek. The left fork is the original roadbed and the one to the right, added later, went down Squalicum Creek to the salt water. The left fork climbed up out of the valley and reached the higher ground in the area of Safeway, called "Summit" on the original line. (M. Impero)

SQUALICUM CREEK BRIDGE NEAR HANNEGAN ROAD
This location is at the point that the creek crosses under Hannegan Road near where the two rail tracks split. (M. Impero)

TRESTLE BRIDGE ON SQUALICUM CREEK ROUTE
This abandoned trestle borders the Bellingham Country Club Golf Course. (M. Impero)

REMNANT OF THE WARNICK BRIDGE

Warnick was one of JJ's top surveyors, and he ran the line to Glacier and beyond. Upon crossing the river approximately four miles below Glacier, a timber trestle bridge was constructed. On the east side was the location of the Warnick Depot, located on the Steiner Homestead. The Warnick Lumber Mill was situated here as well. This stone-built abutment on the west side is the only remaining part of the original bridge. (M. Impero)

GLACIER TRAIN STATION, 2020

The Glacier Station still exists today as a private home. It was moved south about 200 feet from its original location to behind Graham's Store and turned 90 degrees. (M. Impero)

GLACIER STATION AGENT HOUSE
This restored beautiful home in Glacier was the last Glacier Station Agent
House - a far change from the original house shown in Chapter 6. (M. Impero)

CHICAGO, MILWAUKEE, ST. PAUL, AND PACIFIC AT GLACIER
This original sign is currently located to the right of the ticket window of the
former Glacier Train Station. (M. Impero)

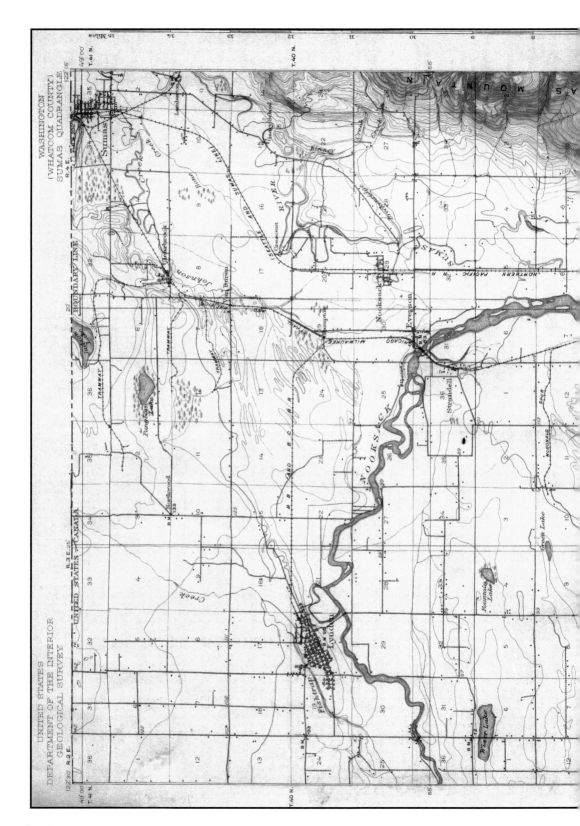

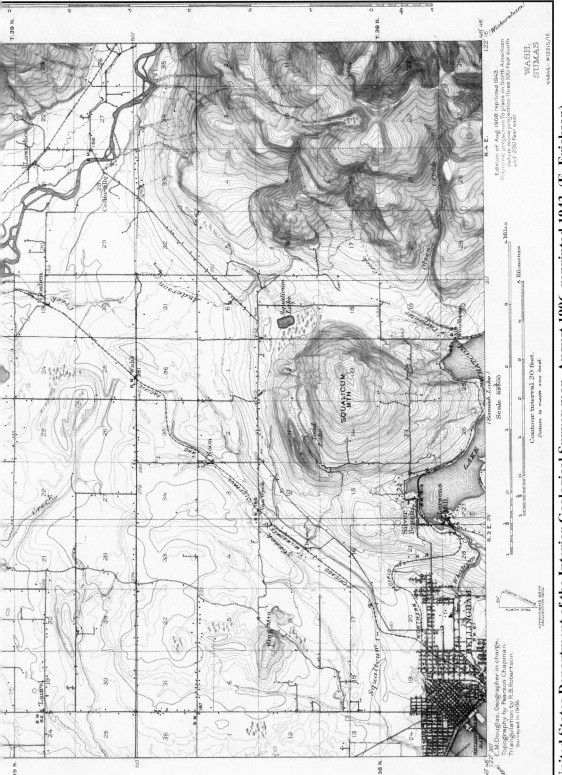

United States Department of the Interior Geological Survey map, August 1906, reprinted 1943. (E. Erickson)